THE COMPLETE NINJA AIR FRYER COOKBOOK 2021

1000-Day Simple, Tasty and Easy Air Fried Recipes for Smart People on A Budget | Bake, Grill, Fry and Roast with Your Ninja Air Fryer | A 4-Week Meal Plan

Dr. Linda Amanda

Contents

INTRODUCTION

Obesity is a worldwide epidemic and a major contribution to the problem is the consumption of fried foods. The delicious taste of fried foods is certainly addictive however, the consumption can lead to the accumulation of unhealthy body fat and body weight. This accumulation does not just mean gaining extra weight. Being overweight also means there is an increased probability that the individual will suffer from other health problems like type 2 diabetes, liver and kidney problems and mental health issues like depression.

Therefore it is no surprise that many formal eating plans encourage the elimination of fried foods from the diet to gain a healthier lifestyle. The idea certainly has merit but what if I told you there was a way to eat healthily while still enjoying fried foods? There is, in fact, a way.

Introducing the Ninja Air Fryer. This is a cutting-edge tool that allows you to continue to enjoy eating "fried" foods without suffering the negative health consequences such as increased cholesterol, elevated blood pressure and increased risk of developing cardiovascular diseases. I will give you all the details on how this amazing machine works, where you can get it and how you can use it.

Also, this book is jam-packed with 100 satisfying recipes to delight your taste buds and keep your body healthy and slim. These recipes include main dishes, side dishes, snacks, desserts and more. The book even includes vegan-friendly and vegetarian-friendly recipes along with a 4-week meal plan and a shopping list to make your life easier.

It is time to say goodbye to oil-laden foods that fill your body with unhealthy calories and body fat and say hello to "fried" foods that are crisp, delicious and good for your waistline. Turn the page to find out more.

Chapter 1. Essentials of Ninja Air Fryer

What is the Ninja Air Fryer?

The Ninja Air Fryer is a special appliance that allows the preparation of your favorite foods via the circulation of hot air. The circulation allows the food to achieve a crisp and golden finish every time. In other words, this appliance allows you to fry food without the excess oil. This is great news because everyone can now enjoy the alternate healthy version to their preferred foods like fried chicken. In addition to "frying" foods, you can also use the Ninja Air Fryer to roast, bake, reheat and dehydrate foods quick and easy.

Why the Ninja Air Fryer?

There is nothing else on the market that astonishes users quite like the Ninja Air Fryer. It allows you to enjoy your favorite fried foods by blowing hot air on them rather than using grease, which coats the food in unhealthy oil. The built-in fan circulates hot air around the food so that it is crisp and crunchy on the outside while being cooked to perfection on the inside. The food appliance also drains oil while it cooks the food. In fact, cooking with the Ninja Air Fryer allows you to enjoy food that is 80% less greasy than food that is traditionally fried in oil. Not only does this appliance prevent unhealthy grease from entering your stomach but it also saves you elbow grease as cleanup is a breeze.

The Ninja Air Fryer also saves you money. This appliance heats up in mere minutes so that you can move from room temperature to cooking temperature quickly and efficiently, which saves you time and money on your electricity bill.

Is the Ninja Air Fryer Better Than a Normal Air Fryer?

The Ninja Air Fryer is a superior buy because of the efficiency with which it cooks food. It uses advanced technology to circulate hot air over and around food at a high speed so that food cooks to a crispy outer finish while ensuring the juices remain in the food so that the inside is soft, tender and full of flavor.

How Does the Ninja Air Fryer Work?

The Ninja Air Fryer is able to achieve such yummy feats through two chemical processes. The first is called caramelization. This process involves the breakdown of sugars found on the exterior of foods. This breakdown is facilitated by the high temperature (between 230 and 360 degrees Fahrenheit) within the air fryer. The breakdown of sugar is what causes the browning of the cooked food.

The second process is called the Maillard reaction. This is a chemical reaction that also causes browning of food. It also reduces sugar to give the distinctive flavor that fried foods have. This occurs between the temperatures of 280 and 330 degrees Fahrenheit.

Models of the Ninja Air Fryer

You have several Ninja Air Fryers options to choose from. The models include:

- AF101
- AF100
- AF101C
- AF101CCO
- AF160
- AF161

Buttons and Functions

The Ninja Air Fryer has many functions and the accompanying buttons. They include:

- **Air broil.** Caramelizes and browns food.
- **Air fry.** Makes food crisp and crunchy with little or no oil.
- **Air roast.** Functions as a roaster oven.
- **Bake**. Creates baked foods.
- **Dehydrate.** Removes the moisture from fruits, veggies and meats.
- **Max crisp**. Used to give food an extra crunch.
- **Reheat**. Gently warms leftover food.

How to Use the Ninja Air Fryer

First, turn on the air fryer unit using the power button. Select the function you would like to perform by pressing the button. Preheat the air fryer by selecting the temperature. This is not available on the Max Crisp function. Next, select the cooking time.

Add the food to the air fryer basket then press the START/STOP button. Halfway through the cooking process, toss or flip the food for even cooking. The timer will pause automatically during that time.

Remove the food when the air fryer beeps. Use mittens or tongs to do this to prevent from getting burned.

Where to Shop for the Ninja Air Fryer

This can be purchased at major online retailers such as Amazon.com or in stores like Target.

Safety Guide for Using the Ninja Air Fryer

Here are a few tips for safe usage of the Ninja Air Fryer:

- Do not allow children to use this appliance unsupervised.
- Ensure the air fryer is properly assembled before use.
- Do not place the air fryer near the edge of a worktop when in use.
- Ensure the basket is securely closed before use.
- Do not use this air fryer for deep frying.

Amazing Tips and Tricks for Using the Ninja Air Fryer

Here are a few general cooking tips to allow you to get the most out of the Ninja Air Fryer:

- Any baking dish or bowl can be inserted into the ninja air fryer as long as it fits correctly. Do not force odd-shaped baking dishes or baking dishes that are too big into the ninja air fryer.

- Parchment paper and aluminum foil are safe to use in the ninja air fryer.
- Do not overcrowd the air fryer basket. Overcrowding will diminish the flavor of your dishes as it prevents even cooking.
- You can open the ninja air fryer at any time to check the doneness of your food just like you would with a traditional oven.
- Water can be added to drawer of the Ninja Air Fryer to prevent from getting smoky-flavored food.
- Lightly coat the food to be air fried in a healthy oil like olive oil for better cooking results.

FAQs

What is the highest temperature selection?

The highest cooking temperature available for Max Crisp and Air Broil are 450 degrees Fahrenheit. All other functions have a maximum temperature of 400 degrees Fahrenheit.

How long does it take to preheat the Ninja Air Fryer?

This is typically no more than 3 minutes. For best cooking results, add the food after the unit has been preheated.

Can I air fry frozen foods?

Yes, you can but for best results, follow a recipe or the package instructions of the particular food.

Can I cook battered food in the Ninja Air Fryer?

Yes, you can. Be sure to use the appropriate dish that fits neatly in the air fryer to do this.

I noticed that some ingredients flew around in the Ninja Air Fryer while in use. Why?

The air fryer uses a high-performance fan to circulate heat in the unit. Therefore, loose ingredients will be blown if not secured. Secure lightweight food with a toothpick.

AIR FRYER COOKING CHART FOR THE AF100 SERIES NINJA AIR FRYER

Beef

Item	Quantity	Preparation	Toss in Oil?	Temperature	Cook Time (mins.)
Burgers	4 quarter-pound patties, 80% lean	1" thick	No	375 °F	8-10
Steaks	2 steaks (8 oz. each)	Whole	No	390 °F	10-12

Fish and Seafood

Item	Quantity	Preparation	Toss in Oil?	Temperature	Cook Time (mins.)
Crab cakes	2 cakes (6-8 oz. each)	None	Yes	350 °F	12-15
Lobster tails	4 tails (3-4 oz. each)	Whole	No	375 °F	5-8
Salmon fillets	2 fillets C 4 oz. each)	None	Yes	390 °F	10-13
Shrimp	16 large	Whole, peeled, tails on	Yes	390 °F	7-10

Pork and Lamb

Item	Quantity	Preparation	Toss in Oil?	Temperature	Cook Time (mins.)
Bacon	4 strips, cut in ha lf	None	No	350 °F	8-10
Pork chops	2 thick-cut, bone-in chops (10-12 ounces each)	Bone in	Yes	375 °F	15-17
	4 boneless chops (8 ounces	Boneless	Yes	375 °F	14-17

	each)				
Pork tenderloins	2 tenderloins (1-1 1/2 lbs. each)	Whole	Yes	375 °F	25-35
Sausages	4 sausages	Whole	No	390 °F	8-10

Poultry

Item	Quantity	Preparation	Toss in Oil?	Temperature	Cook Time (mins.)
Chicken breasts	2 breasts (3/4-1 1f2 lbs. each)	Bone in	Yes	375 °F	25-35
	2 breasts (1/2-3/4 lb. each)	Boneless	Yes	375 °F	18-22
Chicken thighs	4 thighs (6-10 oz. each)	Bone in	Yes	390 °F	22-28
	4 thighs (4-8 oz. each)	Boneless		390 °F	18-22
Chicken wings	21bs	Drumettes & flats	Yes	390 °F	22-26

Vegetables

Item	Quantity	Preparation	Toss in Oil?	Temperature	Cook Time (mins.)
Asparagus	1 bunch	Whole, trim stems	2 tsp	390 °F	8-12
Beets	2 lb.	Whole	No	390 °F	45-60
Bell peppers	4 peppers	Whole	No	400 °F	25-30
Broccoli	1 head	Cut in 1" florets	1 tbsp.	390 °F	10-12
Brussels sprouts	1 lb.	Halved, remove stem	1 tbsp.	390 °F	15-20
Butternut squash	1 to 1 ½ lb.	Cut in 1" pieces	1 tbsp.	390 °F	20-25
Carrots	1 lb.	Peel, Cut in ½" pieces	1 tbsp.	390 °F	13-16
Cauliflower	1 head	Cut in 1" florets	1 tbsp.	390 °F	15-20
Corn on the cob	4 ears	Whole ears, remove husks	1 tbsp.	390 °F	12-15
Green beans	12 oz.	Trim	1 tbsp.	390 °F	8-10
Kale	6 cups, packed	Remove stems,	No	300 °F	8-10

		tear into pieces			
Mushrooms	8 oz.	Rinse, cut into quarters	1 tbsp.	390°F	7-9
Russet potatoes	1 ½ lbs.	1" wedges	1 tbsp.	390°F	18-20
	1 lb.	Thin cut fries	½-3 tbsp.	390°F	20-24
	1 lb.	Thick cut fries	½-3 tbsp.	390°F	23-26
	8 oz.	Pierce with fork 3 times	No	390°F	30-35
Sweet potatoes	1 ½ lbs.	Cut in 1" pieces	1 tbsp.	390°F	15-20
	8 oz.	Pierce with fork 3 times	No	390°F	30-35
Zucchini	1 lb.	Cut in quarters lengthwise, then slice in 1" pieces	1 tbsp.	390°F	15-18

DEHYDRATE CHART FOR THE AF100 SERIES NINJA AIR FRYERS

Item	Preparation Instructions	Temperature	Dehydration Time
Fruits and Vegetables			
Apples	Remove core, create 1/4" slices, rinse in diluted lemon juice, pat dry	135 °F	7-8 hours
Asparagus	Create " pieces, blanch	135 °F	6-8 hours
Bananas	Peel, create 3/8" slices	135 °F	8-10 hours
Beets	Peel, create 1/8" slices	135 °F	6-8 hours
Eggplant	Peel, create ¼" slices, blanch	135 °F	6-8 hours
Fresh Herbs	Rinse, pat dry, remove stems	135 °F	4 hours
Ginger root	Create 3/8" slices	135 °F	6 hours
Mangoes	Peel, create 3/8" slices, remove pit	135 °F	6-8 hours
Mushrooms	Clean with a soft brush	135 °F	6-8 hours
Pineapple	Peel, core, Create 3/8" to ½" slices	135 °F	6-8 hours
Strawberries	Cut in half or create ½" slices	135 °F	6-8 hours
Tomatoes	Create 3/8" slices	135 °F	6-8 hours
Meat, Poultry and Fish			
Beef	Create 1/4" slices, marinate overnight	150 °F	5-7 hours
Chicken	Create 1/4" slices, marinate	150 °F	5-7 hours

	overnight			
Turkey	Create 1/4" slices, marinate overnight	150 °F	5-7 hours
Salmon	Create 1/4" slices, marinate overnight	150 °F	5-7 hours

AIR FRY COOKING CHART FOR THE AF160 SERIES NINJA AIR FRYER

Beef

Item	Quantity	Preparation	Toss in Oil?	Temperature	Cook Time (mins.)
Burgers	4 quarter-pound patties, 80% lean	1" thick	No	375 °F	8-10
Steaks	2 steaks (8 oz. each)	Whole	No	390 °F	10-12

Fish and Seafood

Item	Quantity	Preparation	Toss in Oil?	Temperature	Cook Time (mins.)
Crab cakes	2 cakes (6-8 oz. each)	None	Yes	350 °F	12-15
Lobster tails	4 tails (3-4 oz. each)	Whole	No	375 °F	5-8
Salmon fillets	2 fillets C 4 oz. each)	None	Yes	390 °F	10-13
Shrimp	16 large	Whole, peeled, tails on	Yes	390 °F	9-11

Pork and Lamb

Item	Quantity	Preparation	Toss in Oil?	Temperature	Cook Time (mins.)
Bacon	4 strips, cut in ha lf	None	No	350 °F	8-10

Pork chops	2 thick-cut, bone-in chops (10-12 ounces each)	Bone in	Yes	375 °F	14
	4 boneless chops (8 ounces each)	Boneless	Yes	375 °F	14-17
Pork tenderloins	2 tenderloins (1-1 1/2 lbs. each)	Whole	Yes	375 °F	25-30
Sausages	6 sausages	Whole	No	390 °F	8-10

Poultry

Item	Quantity	Preparation	Toss in Oil?	Temperature	Cook Time (mins.)
Chicken breasts	2 breasts (3/4-1 1/2 lbs. each)	Bone in	Yes	375 °F	25-35
	2 breasts (1/2-3/4 lb. each)	Boneless	Yes	375 °F	18-22
Chicken thighs	4 thighs (6-10 oz. each)	Bone in	Yes	390 °F	22-28
	4 thighs (4-8 oz. each)	Boneless		390 °F	18-22
Chicken wings	3 lbs	Drumettes & flats	Yes	390 °F	22-26

Vegetables

Item	Quantity	Preparation	Toss in Oil?	Temperature	Cook Time (mins.)
Asparagus	2 bunches	Whole, trim stems	2 tsp	390 °F	11-13
Beets	2 lb.	Whole	No	390 °F	45-60
Bell peppers	4 peppers	Whole	No	400 °F	26-30
Broccoli	1 head	Cut in 1" florets	1 tbsp.	390 °F	13-16
Brussels sprouts	2 lbs.	Halved, remove stem	1 tbsp.	390 °F	18-22
Butternut squash	2 lbs.	Cut in 1" pieces	1 tbsp.	390 °F	23-26
Carrots	2 lbs.	Peel, Cut in ½" pieces	1 tbsp.	400 °F	20-24
Cauliflower	2 heads	Cut in 1" florets	1 tbsp.	390 °F	20-24
Corn on the cob	4 ears	Whole ears, remove husks	1 tbsp.	390 °F	12-15
Green beans	12 oz.	Trim	1 tbsp.	390 °F	12-14

Kale	8 oz.	Remove stems, tear into pieces	No	300 °F	8-10
Mushrooms	10 oz.	Rinse, cut into quarters	1 tbsp.	390°F	10-12
Russet potatoes	2 lbs.	1" wedges	1 tbsp.	390°F	20-25
	1 lb.	Thin cut fries	½-3 tbsp.	390°F	20-24
	2 lb.	Thick cut fries	½-3 tbsp.	390°F	23-26
	8 oz.	Pierce with fork 3 times	No	390°F	30-35
Sweet potatoes	2 lbs.	Cut in 1" pieces	1 tbsp.	390°F	20-24
	8 oz.	Pierce with fork 3 times	No	390°F	30-35
Zucchini	2 lbs.	Cut in quarters lengthwise, then slice in 1" pieces	1 tbsp.	390°F	18-20

Max Crisp Cooking Chart for the AF160 Series Ninja Air Fryers

Item	Quantity	Preparation	Toss in Oil?	Cook Time (mins.)
Chicken nuggets	12 oz.	None	None	7-9
Chicken wings	32 oz.	None	1 tbsp.	25
French fries	16 oz.	None	None	15
French fries	32 oz.	None	None	25
Mini corn dogs	14 oz.	None	None	6
Mini corn dogs	24 oz.	None	None	8-10
Mozzarella sticks	24 oz.	None	None	6-8
Pizza rolls	20 oz.	None	None	6-8
Pot stickers	24 oz.	None	None	8-10

*Note that there is no temperature adjustment available for the Max Crisp function.

CHAPTER 2. A HEALTHY 4-WEEK NINJA AIR FRYER MEAL PLAN

REGULAR SHOPPING LIST

The following shopping list is one of a well-stocked kitchen for a household that does not follow vegan of vegetarian practices. It will allow you to prepare the dishes listed below and the recipes to come in the following chapters. Feel free to add and remove items to suit your tastes and preferences. To ensure that your kitchen is always well-stocked, it is best to meal prep. Meal prepping is the process of partially or fully preparing your meals ahead of time. By meal prepping you will gather the recipes that you plan to use that week or month and so, plan your grocery shopping accordingly.

In keeping with a healthy eating plan, try to stick with the healthy options. For example, even commonly considered unhealthy items like butter has low fat options.

PANTRY STAPLES

Olive oil, all-purpose flour, salt, black pepper, ketchup, mustard, cornstarch, brown, sugar, chocolate chips, maple syrup, white vinegar, balsamic vinegar, apple cider vinegar, healthy oils like sesame oil and avocado oil, vanilla extract, active dry yeast, nutritional yeast, baking powder, baking soda, honey, pasta, rice, quinoa, bread crumbs, corn flakes, hummus, salsa

FREEZER AND REFRIGERATOR ITEMS

Butter, eggs, Parmesan cheese, mozzarella cheese, cheddar cheese, cream cheese, ricotta cheese, buttermilk, mayonnaise, plain yogurt

RED MEAT, POULTRY AND SEAFOOD

Scallions, shrimp, salmon, chicken variety, turkey variety, pork variety, lamb variety, steak variety

DRIED HERBS AND SPICES

Cayenne pepper, Italian seasoning, paprika, dried thyme, dried rosemary, garlic powder, onion powder, ground cinnamon, dried oregano, sea salt, sesame seeds, red pepper flakes, chili powder

FRESH HERBS AND SPICES

Parsley, sage, thyme, rosemary, dill, oregano

GRAINS

Brown rice, quinoa, tortillas, popcorn, whole grain pasta, whole grain cereal, oats, whole grain bread, wild rice, bulgur, barley

PRODUCE AND VEGETABLES (FRESH AND FROZEN)

Potatoes, sweet potatoes, beets, mushrooms, bell peppers, yellow onions, green onions, garlic, Brussel sprouts, fresh ginger, scallions, celery, carrots, lettuce, green leafy veggies like spinach, kale and bok choy, cauliflower, broccoli, cucumbers, corn, cabbage, asparagus, bean sprouts

FRUITS (FRESH, FROZEN AND DRIED)

Avocado, pear, apples, dates, fresh and frozen berries, citrus fruits, grapes, apricots, plums, pineapple, raisins, watermelon, mangos, kiwis, prunes, bananas, cherries

SEEDS, NUTS AND LEGUMES

Chia seeds, sunflower seeds, pumpkin seeds, peanuts, cashew nuts, Brazil nuts, flax seeds, walnuts, pecans, almonds, macadamia nuts, pine nuts, hemp seeds, chickpeas, black eye peas, black beans, lentils

DRY AND CANNED FOODS

Canned tomatoes, tomato paste, coconut milk, stocks, broths, canned beans, nuts and seed butters like hazelnut butter and almond butter, tomato sauce, marinara sauce

SHOPPING LIST FOR VEGANS AND VEGETARIANS

Veganism and vegetarianism are two terms that are often confused to mean the same thing but they are in fact different. Vegetarianism involves avoiding the consumption of meat and animal products but still making allowances for the consumption of dairy products like milk and eggs. Veganism, on the other hand, restricts all animal and animal by-products from the diet including eggs and milk.

To accommodate for a vegetarian diet, you can consume all of the products in the shopping list above except for the animal products exempting eggs and milk. The products that will be mentioned hereafter are safe for both vegan and vegetarian diets. Due to the lack of consumption of meat, poultry and other animal by-products, vegans and vegetarians need to supplement their diet with protein substitutes such as tofu, miso and tempeh.

Here is a list of items that can be used for the substitution of dairy and eggs:

- Applesauce and crushed bananas can be used to substitute eggs. 1 tablespoon plus 3 tablespoons of water can also be used to substitute one egg.
- Buttermilk can be substituted by adding 1 tablespoon of lemon juice to one cup of non-dairy milk.
- Common dairy milk substitutes include almond milk, hemp milk rice milk oat milk, flax milk, soya milk and coconut milk. These are all nondairy milks.
- Coconut oil, olive oil and canola oil are good substitutes for butter.
- Dairy yoghurt substitutes include cashew yoghurt, almond yoghurt and coconut yoghurt.

It should also be noted that there are vegan and vegetarian friendly substitutes for many other dairy items like vegan butter, vegan cheese, vegan margarine and vegan cream cheese.

4-WEEK NINJA AIR FRY MEAL PLAN

WEEK 1

Day 1

Breakfast: Blueberries Wheat Pancakes

Lunch: Chicken Tenders and Tahini Sauce

Dinner: Catfish and Green Beans

Snack 1: Air Fried Popcorn

Snack 2: Avocado Fries

Day 2

Breakfast: Breakfast Frittata

Lunch: Coconut Shrimp

Dinner: Salmon and Broccoli

Snack 1: Brussels Sprouts Chips

Snack 2: Berry Pop Tarts

Day 3

Breakfast: Veggie Omelette

Lunch: Stir Fried Beef Veggie Noodles

Dinner: Lamb Chops and Snow Peas

Snack 1: French Fries

Snack 2: Boiled Eggs

Day 4

Breakfast: Bacon and Eggs

Lunch: Rotisserie Chicken

Dinner: Herbed Lamb Chop and Veggies

Snack 1: Ranch Kale Chips

Snack 2: Cheese Sticks

Day 5

Breakfast: Loaded Hash Browns

Lunch: Zucchini Fritters

Dinner: Stuffed Mushrooms

Snack 1: Spicy Plantain Chips

Snack 2: Milk Beignets

Day 6

Breakfast: Breakfast Casserole

Lunch: Healthy French Fries

Dinner: Korean Chicken Wings

Snack 1: Cauliflower Tots

Snack 2: Pickle Fries

Day 7

Breakfast: Spinach Quiche

Lunch: Asian Fried Cauliflower

Dinner: Pork Roast

Snack 1: Cinnamon Roll

Snack 2: Fried Pickles

WEEK 2

Day 1

Breakfast: Cheesy Breakfast Bake

Lunch: Popcorn Chicken

Dinner: Air Fried Pork Chops and Brussel Sprout Fries

Snack 1: Churros

Snack 2: Sweet Potato Tots

Day 2

Breakfast: Meat and Veggies Egg Bites

Lunch: Baked Potato

Dinner: Italian Herb Pork Loin

Snack 1: Mozzarella Sticks

Snack 2: Baked Pear

Day 3

Breakfast: Breakfast Potatoes

Lunch: Chicken Taquitos

Dinner: Steak and Mashed Potatoes

Snack 1: Brownies

Snack 2: Berry Muffin

Day 4

Breakfast: Baked Apple with Maple Syrup and Toasted Walnuts

Lunch: Pepperoni Pizza

Dinner: Lemon Salmon

Snack 1: Pizza Bites

Snack 2: Maple Donut

Day 5

Breakfast: Cinnamon Rolls

Lunch: Cheese Burger

Dinner: Shrimp and Sausage

Snack 1: Baked Peach

Snack 2: Granola

Day 6

Breakfast: Cranberry Almond Muffins

Lunch: Hot Dogs with Cheese

Dinner: Chicken Parmesan

Snack 1: Baked Fruit Bowl

Snack 2: Zucchini Chips

Day 7

Breakfast: Green Apple Donuts

Lunch: Chicken Tortillas

Dinner: Cajun Shrimp

Snack 1: Oat Raisin Cookies

Snack 2: Cinnamon Cheesecake

WEEK 3

Day 1

Breakfast: Homemade Pop Tarts

Lunch: Cauliflower Rice Balls

Dinner: Roast Chicken Dinner

Snack 1: Molten Lava Cake

Snack 2: Cranberry Oat Bars

Day 2

Breakfast: French Toast with Maple Syrup

Lunch: Baked Sweet Potatoes

Dinner: Honey Garlic Pork Chops

Snack 1: S'more popcorn

Snack 2: Candied Walnuts

Day 3

Breakfast: Egg Tarts

Lunch: Chickpea Tacos

Dinner: Steak Bites with Mushrooms

Snack 1: Caramel Popcorn

Snack 2: Apple Pie Roll Ups

Day 4

Breakfast: Pumpkin Muffin

Lunch: Naan Pizza

Dinner: Ham Crescent Rolls

Snack 1: Cheese Biscuits

Snack 2: Banana Oat Cupcake

Day 5

Breakfast: Broccoli Quiche

Lunch: Shrimp Spring Rolls

Dinner: Curry Chickpeas Dinner

Snack 1: Kale Chips

Snack 2: Chocolate Chip Cookies

Day 6

Breakfast: Breakfast Biscuit Bombs

Lunch: Greek Feta Fries

Dinner: Pork Dumplings

Snack 1: Potato Chips

Snack 2: Cinnamon Sugar Pecans

Day 7

Breakfast: Fried Egg and Toast

Lunch: Quesadillas

Dinner: Sweet n' Spicy Pork Chops with Potato Wedges

Snack 1: Dehydrated Banana Chips

Snack 2: Candied Peanuts

WEEK 4

Day 1

Breakfast: Breakfast Sausage and Eggs

Lunch: Turkey Meatballs with Sautéed Veggies

Dinner: Roasted Salmon Dinner

Snack 1: Vanilla Donuts

Snack 2: Sweet Potato Fries and Tahini

Day 2

Breakfast: Ginger Spice Pancakes

Lunch: Empanadas

Dinner: Fried Chicken and Sweet Potato Fries

Snack 1: Hand Pie

Snack 2: Apple Chips

Day 3

Breakfast: Egg White Omelette

Lunch: Meaty Calzone

Dinner: Fish and Chips

Snack 1: Cinnamon Biscuits

Snack 2: Plantain Chips

Day 4

Breakfast: Baked Avocado Eggs

Lunch: Pita Pizza

Dinner: Roast Beef

Snack 1: Beet Chips

Snack 2: Chocolate Cheesecake

Day 5

Breakfast: Breakfast Loaded Bell Peppers

Lunch: Spanakopita Bites

Dinner: Rosemary Lamb

Snack 1: Buffalo-Flavored Cauliflower Bites

Snack 2: Sweet Potato Chips

Day 6

Breakfast: Sausage Lasagna

Lunch: Toasted Sesame Tofu

Dinner: Mongolian Beef

Snack 1: Apple Cinnamon Chips

Snack 2: Onion Rings

Day 7

Breakfast: Vegetarian Breakfast Casserole

Lunch: Avocado and Egg

Dinner: Leg of Lamb

Snack 1: Corn Dogs

Snack 2: Air Fried Corn on the Cob

MEASUREMENT CONVERSIONS

The recipes that will be detailed in the coming chapters will be using measurements in pounds (lb.), ounces (oz.), cups, teaspoons (tsp) and tablespoons (tbsp.). To accommodate all who will enjoy this cookbook, here is a useful conversion cheat sheet to help you easily recreate this recipes:

CAPACITY CONVERSIONS

1 tablespoons = 3 teaspoons = 15 milliliters

2 tablespoons = 1 ounces = 30 milliliters

¼ cup = 4 tablespoons = 2 ounces = 12 teaspoons

½ cup = 8 tablespoons = 4 ounces

1 cup = 8 ounces = 16 tablespoons

2 cups = 1 pint = 950 milliliters

4 cups = 1 quart

WEIGHT CONVERSIONS

1 ounce = 28 grams

1 pound = 454 grams

TEMPERATURE CONVERSIONS

Also note that temperatures will be expressed in degrees Fahrenheit (F) but if you refer, here is a list of degrees Celsius (C) conversions:

100 °F = 37 °C

150 °F = 65 °C

200 °F = 93 °C

250 °F = 121 °C

300 °F = 150 °C

325 °F = 160 °C

350 °F = 180 °C

375 °F = 190 °C

400 °F = 200 °C

Chapter 3. Breakfast and Lunch Recipes

Breakfast Recipes

Blueberries Wheat Pancakes

Prep Time: 5 minutes/ Cook Time 10 minutes/ Serves: 6

Ingredients:

- 1 cup whole wheat flour
- 1 cup coconut milk
- 3 eggs, lightly beaten
- ¼ cup applesauce
- A pinch of salt
- Optional: maple syrup to garnish

Directions:

1. Preheat the Ninja Air Fryer to 350 degrees F and spray a cast iron tray with nonstick spray.
2. Mix all the ingredients in a large bowl. Blend to a smooth and fluid consistency.
3. Pour the batter into the cast iron tray and air fry for 8 to 10 minutes. The pancake may be firm to the touch when done but will soften as it cools.
4. Garnish and serve warm.

Nutrition value per serving: Calories: 204 kcal, Carbs: 19.4 g, Fat: 11.9 g, Protein: 5.9 g.

Breakfast Frittata

Prep Time: 10 minutes/ Cook Time 15 minutes/ Serves: 5

Ingredients:

- 5 eggs, lightly beaten
- ¼ cup ground turkey
- ½ cup cheddar cheese, shredded
- 1/3 cup yellow onions, chopped
- 1/3 cup red bell pepper, chopped

Directions:

1. Preheat the Ninja Air Fryer to 360 degrees F and spray a 6x2 baking pan

with nonstick spray.
2. Mix all the ingredients in a large bowl.
3. Pour the mixture into the baking pan and air fry for 20 minutes or until the frittata has set firm. Serve warm.

Nutrition value per serving: Calories: 146 kcal, Carbs: 1.8 g, Fat: 10 g, Protein: 13 g.

VEGGIE OMELETTE

Prep Time: 5 minutes/ Cook Time 10 minutes/ Serves: 5

Ingredients:

- 6 eggs
- ½ cup almond milk
- ¼ cup red bell pepper, chopped,
- ¼ cup mushrooms, chopped
- ¼ cup cheddar cheese, shredded
- ¼ tsp garlic powder
- A pinch of salt

Directions:

1. Preheat the Ninja Air Fryer to 350 degrees F and spray a 6x4 baking pan with nonstick spray.
2. Combine the eggs, salt, garlic powder and almond milk in a small bowl.
3. Add the veggies and mix to incorporate.
4. Pour the mixture into the baking pan and air fry for up to 10 minutes. Halfway through the air frying process, sprinkle the cheese on top of the omelette. Plate the omelet and serve warm with any desired toppings.

Nutrition value per serving: Calories: 157 kcal, Carbs: 2.5 g, Fat: 12.9 g, Protein: 8.8 g.

BACON AND EGGS

Prep Time: 0 minutes/ Cook Time 30 minutes/ Serves: 2

Ingredients:

- 4 large eggs
- 6 bacon strips

Directions:

1. Set the eggs on the center rack of the Ninja Air Fryer and set the air fryer

at a temperature of 260 degrees F. Air fry for no more than 10 minutes for soft boiled eggs. Air fry for no more than 12 minutes for medium boiled eggs. Air fry for no more than 15 minutes for hard boiled eggs.

2. Remove the eggs from the air fryer at the preferred time and place in an ice bath for 2 minutes. Peel the shell, cut the eggs in half and plate.
3. Place the bacon strips on the lowest rack and set the air fryer temperature to 375 degrees F. Air fry for about 15 minutes for extra crispy bacon. Air fry for less time if preferred.
4. Place the bacon next to the eggs and serve.

Nutrition value per serving: Calories: 248 kcal, Carbs: 0.8 g, Fat: 12.9 g, Protein: 30.6 g.

LOADED HASH BROWNS

Prep Time: 35 minutes/ Cook Time 20 minutes/ Serves: 8

Ingredients:

- 5 large russet potatoes
- ½ cup red bell peppers, chopped
- ½ cup green bell peppers, chopped
- ½ cup green onions, chopped
- 1 tsp garlic powder
- 1 tsp onion powder
- 3 tsp olive oil
- Salt and pepper to taste

Directions:

1. Grate the potatoes with a cheese grater. Use the largest holes.
2. Soak the shredded potatoes for 25 minutes in cold water to remove the starch. Removing the starch allows the potatoes to crisp when cooked.
3. Drain the potatoes and place on a paper towel to dry.
4. Preheat the Ninja Air Fryer to 400 degrees F and spray a 6x4 casserole dish with nonstick spray.
5. Placed the dried potatoes in a large bowl and season with the garlic powder, onion powder, olive oil, salt and pepper.
6. Pour the mixture into the dish and air fry for 20 minutes. Halfway through the air frying process, add the veggies and stir the potatoes.
7. Allow to cool then serve.

Nutrition value per serving: Calories: 183 kcal, Carbs: 38.3 g, Fat: 2 g, Protein: 4.2 g.

CHEESY BREAKFAST BAKE

Prep Time: 10 minutes/ Cook Time 20 minutes/ Serves: 3

Ingredients:

- 6 large eggs
- 3 tbsp. almond milk
- 2 whole wheat sliced bread, torn into small equal-sized pieces
- 2 cups baby spinach
- 1/3 cup cheddar cheese, shredded
- ½ cup red bell pepper, diced
- Salt and pepper to taste

Directions:

1. Preheat the Ninja Air Fryer to 250 degrees F and spray a 6x4 baking pan with nonstick spray.
2. Combine the eggs, salt, pepper and almond milk in a small bowl.
3. Fold in the rest of the ingredients.
4. Pour the mixture into the baking pan and air fry for 20 minutes. Allow the bake to cool. Plate the omelet and serve warm with any desired toppings.

Nutrition value per serving: Calories: 286 kcal, Carbs: 12.7 g, Fat: 18.8 g, Protein: 19.5 g.

MEAT AND VEGGIES EGG BITES

Prep Time: 5 minutes/ Cook Time 15 minutes/ Serves: 4

Ingredients:

- 3 large eggs
- 1 tbsp. condensed milk
- ¼ cup cheddar cheese, shredded
- 2 tbsp. Monterey Jack cheese, shredded
- ½ cup bacon, cooked and chopped
- ¼ cup bell peppers
- ¼ cup yellow onions, chopped
- ¼ cup baby spinach
- Salt and pepper to taste

Directions:

1. Preheat the Ninja Air Fryer to 300 degrees F and spray 4 silicon muffin molds with nonstick spray.

2. Combine the eggs, salt, pepper and milk in a small bowl.
3. Fold in the rest of the ingredients.
4. Pour the mixture into the baking pan and air fry for 15 minutes or until a toothpick inserted in the center comes out clean. Allow to cool. Plate and serve warm.

Nutrition value per serving: Calories: 139 kcal, Carbs: 4.5 g, Fat: 13.6 g, Protein: 13.2 g.

BREAKFAST POTATOES

Prep Time: 3 minutes/ Cook Time 15 minutes/ Serves: 3

Ingredients:

- 3 large Yukon Gold potatoes, peeled and cubed to 1-inch squares
- 1 tbsp. olive oil
- ½ tsp garlic powder
- ½ tsp red chili flakes
- Salt and pepper to taste

Directions:

1. Preheat the Ninja Air Fryer to 400 degrees F and spray the air fryer basket with nonstick spray.
2. Toss all the ingredients together and air fry for 15 minutes. Intermittently stop the process to shake the basket to ensure even cooking.
3. Plate and serve with desired sauce.

Nutrition value per serving: Calories: 170 kcal, Carbs: 30.8 g, Fat: 4.9 g, Protein: 3.6 g.

LUNCH RECIPES

TURKEY MEATBALLS WITH SAUT ED VEGGIES

Prep Time: 10 minutes/ Cook Time 10 minutes/ Serves: 6

Ingredients:

- ½ lb. ground turkey
- 2 tbsp. panko breadcrumbs
- 1 tbsp. whole milk
- 1 tbsp. olive oil
- 1 tbsp. onion, finely chopped
- 2 garlic cloves, minced

- 2 tbsp. parsley, chopped
- ½ tbsp. fresh rosemary, chopped
- ½ tbsp. fresh thyme, chopped
- 1 small egg, slightly beaten
- ½ tbsp. Dijon mustard
- Salt and pepper to taste
- Sautéed veggies

Directions:

1. Preheat the Ninja Air Fryer to 400 degrees F.
2. Heat the olive oil in a skillet over medium heat and sauté the onions until translucent. Add the garlic and cook for 1 minute. Remove the mixture from the heat.
3. Combine the panko and milk in a large bowl and set aside for 5 minutes.
4. Add the cooked onions and remaining ingredients except the veggies to the panko mixture. Stir to combine.
5. Shape the mixture into 12 1 ½ inch balls and place in a single layer into the air fryer basket. Air fry for 10 minutes or until the meatballs are light brown. Serve over the sautéed veggies.

Nutrition value per serving: Calories: 121 kcal, Carbs: 3.5 g, Fat: 7.4 g, Protein: 12 g.

AIR FRIED HOT DOGS

Prep Time: 2 minutes/ Cook Time 5 minutes/ Serves: 4

Ingredients:

- 4 hot dogs
- 4 hot dog buns

Directions:

1. Preheat the Ninja Air Fryer to 390 degrees F and place the hot dogs on the center rack of the air fryer. Air fry for 5 minutes.
2. Remove the hot dog and place into the sliced hot dog bun. Add desired toppings. If you added cheese, place the hot dog into the air fryer for 2 more minutes. Serve.

Nutrition value per serving: Calories: 177 kcal, Carbs: 27.2 g, Fat: 2.3 g, Protein: 9.3 g.

ROTISSERIE CHICKEN SALAD

Prep Time: 15 minutes/ Cook Time 20 minutes/ Serves: 8

Ingredients:

- 1 whole chicken, cut into 8 pieces
- 1 tsp garlic powder
- 1 tsp onion powder
- 1 tsp paprika
- 1 tsp dried oregano
- 1 tsp dried thyme
- Veggie mix, cooked
- Salt and pepper to taste

Directions:

1. Preheat the Ninja Air Fryer to 350 degrees F.
2. Combine all the spices then sprinkle over the chicken. Rub the seasoning into the chicken.
3. Place the chicken in the air fryer basket for 20 minutes. Flip halfway through the process. Ensure that the chicken has reached an internal temperature of 165 degrees before serving. Serve with steamed or sautéed veggies. Top with desired sauce.

Nutrition value per serving: Calories: 41 kcal, Carbs: 1.5 g, Fat: 1.4 g, Protein: 5.6 g.

HEALTHY FRENCH FRIES

Prep Time: 10 minutes/ Cook Time 20 minutes/ Serves: 6

Ingredients:

- 4 large russet potatoes, cut into ¼" fries
- 1 tbsp. olive oil
- 3 tbsp. parmesan cheese
- 2 tbsp. parsley, finely chopped
- Salt and pepper to taste

Directions:

1. Ensure that the moisture is removed from the potatoes then mix with all the other ingredients.
2. Place in the Ninja Air Fryer, which was preheated to 360 degrees F. Spread in an even layer and cook for 20 minutes. Flip the fries every 5 minutes using tongs.

3. Serve warm with your favorite sauce such as ketchup.

Nutrition value per serving: Calories: 205 kcal, Carbs: 38.9 g, Fat: 3.6 g, Protein: 5.7 g.

BAKED POTATO

Prep Time: 3 minutes/ Cook Time 40 minutes/ Serves: 2

Ingredients:

- 2 Russet potatoes
- 1 tbsp. olive oil
- 1 tsp parsley, chopped
- 1 garlic clove, minced
- Salt and pepper to taste

Directions:

1. Preheat the Ninja Air Fryer to 390 degrees F.
2. Wash and dry the potatoes.
3. Prick the potatoes all over with a fork to create holes.
4. Mix the rest of the ingredients together in a small bowl then rub the mixture over the potatoes.
5. Air fry the potatoes for 40 minutes or until fork tender.
6. Plate the potatoes, slice down the center and top with desired items.

Nutrition value per serving: Calories: 210 kcal, Carbs: 34 g, Fat: 7.2 g, Protein: 3.7 g.

PEPPERONI PIZZA

Prep Time: 10 minutes/ Cook Time 10 minutes/ Serves: 4

Ingredients:

- 8-oz pizza dough
- ½ tbsp. olive oil
- ¼ cup pizza sauce
- ½ cup mozzarella cheese
- ¼ cup pepperoni

Directions:

1. Preheat the Ninja Air Fryer to 400 degrees F.

2. Roll out the pizza dough in an 8" circle on a clean, floured surface with floured hands.
3. Brush the pizza with the olive oil and layer the pizza sauce, cheese and pepperoni on the dough in that order. Ensure that a border of ½ inch is left uncovered around the pizza.
4. Air fry fo10 minutes or the cheese has melted and the crusted is golden brown.
5. Remove the pizza from the air fryer, garnish as desired, slice and serve.

Nutrition value per serving: Calories: 368 kcal, Carbs: 25.9 g, Fat: 26 g, Protein: 7.6 g.

TURKEY BURGER

Prep Time: 5 minutes/ Cook Time 10 minutes/ Serves: 4

Ingredients:

- 1 lb. ground turkey
- 1 tbsp. soy sauce
- Salt and pepper to taste
- 2 garlic cloves, minced
- 4 hamburger buns, halved and toasted
- Lettuce
- Tomatoes
- Red onions, thinly sliced
- Low-fat mayo

Directions:

1. Preheat the Ninja Air Fryer to 375 degrees F and spray a small baking sheet with nonstick spray.
2. Combine the turkey, soy sauce and garlic in a large bowl.
3. Shape the mixture into 4 patties. Flatten to ½" inch thick circles. Season the patties with salt and pepper.
4. Air fry for 10 minutes. Flip the patties halfway through the process.
5. Spread mayo onto the hamburger buns. Place lettuce on one side then layer with the patties and veggies. Cover with the other bun slice and serve.

Nutrition value per serving: Calories: 369 kcal, Carbs: 27.1 g, Fat: 14.6 g, Protein: 36.1 g.

Chapter 4. Red Meat Recipes

Simple Lamb Chop

Prep Time: 5 minutes/ Cook Time 25 minutes/ Serves: 2

Ingredients:

- 2 medium lamb chops
- 1 tbsp. lemon juice
- 1 tsp dried rosemary
- 1 tsp dried thyme
- Salt and pepper to taste

Directions:

1. Preheat the Ninja Air Fryer to 350 degrees F.
2. Combine all the ingredients to season the lamb chops thoroughly.
3. Place the lamb chops in the air fryer basket for 25 minutes.
4. Allow the lamb chops to rest for 10 minutes before serving.

Nutrition value per serving: Calories: 265 kcal, Carbs: 5.9 g, Fat: 15.2 g, Protein: 25.2 g.

Breaded Pork Chop

Prep Time: 7 minutes/ Cook Time 12 minutes/ Serves: 4

Ingredients:

- 4 5-oz ¾" boneless pork chops, fat trimmed
- ½ cup panko bread crumbs
- 2 tbsp. parmesan cheese, grated
- 1 egg, beaten
- 1 tsp paprika
- ½ tsp garlic powder
- ½ tsp onion powder
- Salt and pepper to taste

Directions:

1. Preheat the Ninja Air Fryer to 400 degrees F and spray the air fryer basket with nonstick spray.
2. Combine the panko bread crumbs, parmesan cheese, salt, pepper,

onion, powder, garlic powder and paprika in a shallow bowl large enough to fit the pork chops.

3. Place the egg in another bowl of the same size.
4. Dip the pork chops into the egg and coat then the panko mixture
5. Place the pork chops into the air fryer and cook for 12 minute. Flip halfway through the process. Serve with your favorite sides.

Nutrition value per serving: Calories: 304 kcal, Carbs: 11.7g, Fat: 15.6 g, Protein: 29.5 g.

BACON-WRAPPED FILET MIGNON

Prep Time: 4 minutes/ Cook Time 15 minutes/ Serves: 4

Ingredients:

- 4 filet mignon steaks
- 4 bacon slices
- Olive oil
- Salt and pepper to taste

Directions:

1. Preheat the Ninja Air Fryer to 380 degrees F.
2. Wrap each filet mignon with a piece of bacon and secure with a toothpick.
3. Sprinkle each steak with salt and pepper then spray with olive oil.
4. Air fry the steaks for 15 minutes, Flip halfway through the process. Serve with your favorite sides.

Nutrition value per serving: Calories: 458 kcal, Carbs: 0 g, Fat: 26.5 g, Protein: 53 g.

STEAK AND POTATOES

Prep Time: 15 minutes/ Cook Time 20 minutes/ Serves: 6

Ingredients:

- 1 lb. steak, cut into ½" squares
- 2 tbsp. olive oil
- 4 medium potatoes, cut into ½" squares and blanched
- 1 tsp Worcestershire sauce
- ½ tbsp. all-purpose seasoning
- Salt and pepper to taste

Directions:

1. Preheat the Ninja Air Fryer to 380 degrees F.
2. Pat the steak pieces dry with paper towels.
3. Toss all the ingredients together then arrange in an even layer in the air fryer basket. Air fry for to up to 20 minutes. Flip the steak and potatoes at least twice during the process.
4. Garnish as desired and serve warm.

Nutrition value per serving: Calories: 289 kcal, Carbs: 22.5 g, Fat: 8.6 g, Protein: 29.7 g.

SIMPLE NEW YORK STEAKS

Prep Time: 4 minutes/ Cook Time 13 minutes/ Serves: 2

Ingredients:

- 1 New York strip steak
- Olive oil
- Salt and pepper to taste

Directions:

1. Preheat the Ninja Air Fryer to 400 degrees F and spray the air fryer basket with nonstick spray.
2. Season the steaks with the salt and pepper and spray with olive oil.
3. Place the steaks in the air fryer basket and cook for 13 minutes. Flip halfway through the process.
4. Serve warm with your preferred sides.

Nutrition value per serving: Calories: 470 kcal, Carbs: 6.5 g, Fat: 7 g, Protein: 14.6 g.

MEATLOAF

Prep Time: 8 minutes/ Cook Time 25 minutes/ Serves: 8

Ingredients:

- 1 lb. ground pork
- 4 tbsp. bread crumbs
- 1 egg, lightly beaten
- 1 tbsp. fresh parsley, chopped
- 1 small yellow onion, chopped

- Olive oil
- Salt and pepper to taste

Directions:

1. Preheat the Ninja Air Fryer to 390 degrees F and spray an 8x4 loaf pan with nonstick spray.
2. Thoroughly combine all the ingredients except the olive oil in a large bowl then transfer to the loaf pan. Brush the top of the meatloaf with olive oil.
3. Place in the air fryer and cook for 25 minutes or until the top is golden brown.
4. Allow the meatloaf to cool for at least 10 minutes before serving.

Nutrition value per serving: Calories: 121 kcal, Carbs: 3.3 g, Fat: 4.5 g, Protein: 16.1 g.

HERBED RIBEYE STEAK

Prep Time: 8 minutes/ Cook Time 14 minutes/ Serves: 2

Ingredients:

- 2 1-lb. bone-in ribeye steaks
- 2 tbsp. butter, softened
- 1 tsp fresh rosemary, chopped
- 1 tsp fresh thyme, chopped
- 1 tsp fresh parsley, chopped
- 2 garlic cloves, minced
- Salt and pepper to taste

Directions:

1. Preheat the Ninja Air Fryer to 400 degrees F.
2. Season the steaks with the salt and pepper.
3. Combine the remaining ingredients in a small bowl then spread onto the steaks.
4. Place the steaks in the air fryer and cook for up to 14 minutes for medium steaks. Flip halfway through the process. Serve with your favorite sides.

Nutrition value per serving: Calories: 480 kcal, Carbs: 1.8 g, Fat: 23.7 g, Protein: 18.4 g.

Italian Herb Pork Chops

Prep Time: 4 minutes/ Cook Time 12 minutes/ Serves: 2

Ingredients:

- 2 1" thick pork chops
- ½ tbsp. Italian seasoning
- 2 tbsp. olive oil

Directions:

1. Combine all the ingredients and allow to marinate in a sealed plastic bag for at least 2 hours.
2. Preheat the air fryer to 350 degrees.
3. Place the pork chops in the air fryer basket and cook for 12 minutes. Flip halfway through the cooking process.
4. Allow the pork chops to sit for at least 5 minutes before serving.

Nutrition value per serving: Calories: 387 kcal, Carbs: 0.4 g, Fat: 34.9 g, Protein: 18 g.

Italian Stuffed Pork Chops

Prep Time: 10 minutes/ Cook Time 12 minutes/ Serves: 4

Ingredients:

- 4 thick cut pork chops
- 4 tbsp. cream cheese
- 1 cup spinach
- ½ cup mozzarella cheese
- ½ tbsp. dried rosemary
- ½ tbsp. dried oregano
- ½ tbsp. garlic powder
- ½ tbsp. onion powder
- 1 tsp paprika
- Salt and pepper to taste

Directions:

1. Preheat the Ninja Air Fryer to 400 degrees F.
2. Butterfly the pork chops using a sharp knife. Season with the salt and pepper.
3. Add all the remaining ingredients to a small bowl and combined

thoroughly.

4. Fill each pork chop with an equal amount of filling.
5. Place the pork chops filling side up in the air fryer and cook for up to 12 minutes. Serve with the desired sides.

Nutrition value per serving: Calories: 378 kcal, Carbs: 3.1 g, Fat: 19.4 g, Protein: 23.4 g.

FRIED PORK CHOPS

Prep Time: 8 minutes/ Cook Time 6 minutes/ Serves: 4

Ingredients:

- 4 pork loin chops
- 1 egg, lightly beaten
- ½ cup all-purpose flour
- ½ cup bread crumbs
- Olive oil
- Salt and pepper to taste

Directions:

1. Preheat the ninja air fryer to 400 degrees F.
2. Season the pork loins with the salt and pepper.
3. Place the flour, egg and breadcrumbs into individual bowls. Each bowl should be shallow and wide so that the pork chops fit neatly in them.
4. Dredge each pork loin into the flour then into the egg and into the breadcrumbs next.
5. Spray the pork chops with olive oil and place into the air fryer basket for 6 minutes. Flip halfway through the process.
6. Allow to cool and serve with your favorite sides.

Nutrition value per serving: Calories: 412 kcal, Carbs: 21.8 g, Fat: 25.3 g, Protein: 22.8 g.

SOUTHERN STYLE PORK CHOPS

Prep Time: 10 minutes/ Cook Time 13 minutes/ Serves: 2

Ingredients:

- 2 pork chops
- 2 tbsp. buttermilk
- 1/3 cup all-purpose flour

- 1 tbsp. pork seasoning
- Salt and pepper to taste

Directions:

1. Marinate the pork chops by placing the pork chops, buttermilk and seasoning in a sealable plastic bag. Place in the refrigerator for 30 minutes.
2. Season the flour with the salt and pepper and liberally coat each pork chop. Allow this to sit for 10 minutes.
3. Preheat the ninja air fryer to 400 degrees F.
4. Place the pork chops in the air fryer basket and cook for 13 minutes. Flip half way through the process.
5. Allow the pork chops to sit for at least 10 minutes before serving.

Nutrition value per serving: Calories: 378 kcal, Carbs: 21.5 g, Fat: 21 g, Protein: 24.1 g.

HERBED RACK OF LAMB

Prep Time: 7 minutes/ Cook Time 10 minutes/ Serves: 4

Ingredients:

- 1 rack of lamb
- 3 tbsp. olive oil
- 1 tbsp. dried rosemary
- 1 tbsp. dried thyme
- 2 garlic cloves, minced
- Salt and pepper to taste

Directions:

1. Preheat the ninja air fryer to 360 degrees F.
2. Combine all the ingredients except the rack of lamb in a small bowl to form the seasoning.
3. Rub the mixture all over the rack of lamb and place the rack of lamb into the air fryer basket. Cook for 10-minutes and check the internal temperature. For rare meat, the internal temperature should be 145 degrees F. For medium meat, the internal temperature should be 160 degrees F. For well-done meat, the internal temperature should be 170 degrees F.
4. Serve with your favorite sides after the lamb has rested for a minimum of 10 minutes.

Nutrition value per serving: Calories: 287 kcal, Carbs: 1.5 g, Fat: 20.7 g, Protein: 23.2 g.

RIBLETS

Prep Time: 4 minutes/ Cook Time 12 minutes/ Serves: 5

Ingredients:

- ½ lb. pork riblets, divided into single pieces with bones
- 1 tbsp. soy sauce
- ½ tsp oyster sauce
- 1 tbsp. ketchup
- 1 tbsp. dry sherry
- 1 tbsp. sugar
- 6 garlic cloves, halved

Directions:

1. Combine all the ingredients and allow the riblets to marinate in a sealable plastic bag for at least 2 hours.
2. Preheat the ninja air fryer to 360 degrees F.
3. Add the riblets into the air fryer basket and cook for 12 minutes. Flip half way through.
4. Garnish as desired and serve with your favorite dipping sauce.

Nutrition value per serving: Calories: 411 kcal, Carbs: 18.7 g, Fat: 27 g, Protein: 19.5 g.

BBQ-FLAVORED BABY BACK RIBS

Prep Time: 6 minutes/ Cook Time 20 minutes/ Serves: 5

Ingredients:

- 1 rack of baby back ribs
- ½ tsp brown sugar
- 1 tbsp. liquid smoke
- 1 tbsp. olive oil
- 1 tsp cayenne pepper
- 1 tsp onion powder
- 1 tsp garlic powder
- Salt and pepper to taste
- Barbecue sauce

Directions:

1. Preheat the ninja air fryer to 400 degrees F.
2. Ensure that the ribs have been dried then rub with the olive oil and liquid smoke.
3. Mix all the remaining ingredients except for the rack of baby back ribs and the barbecue sauce in a small bowl to create the seasoning.
4. Season the ribs and place into the air fryer basket. Cook for 20 minutes.
5. Brush the ribs with BBQ sauce once it is done cooking. Serve.

Nutrition value per serving: Calories: 479 kcal, Carbs: 5.2 g, Fat: 32.5 g, Protein: 0.2 g.

LEG OF LAMB

Prep Time: 5 minutes/ Cook Time 40 minutes/ Serves: 5

Ingredients:

- 1 leg of lamb
- Salt and pepper to taste

Directions:

1. Preheat the ninja air fryer to 360 degrees F.
2. Season the leg of lamb with the salt and pepper then place in the air fryer basket. Cook for 40 minutes.
3. Serve warm with desired sides

Nutrition value per serving: Calories: 243 kcal, Carbs: 0 g, Fat: 9.6 g, Protein: 36. g.

Chapter 5. Poultry Recipes

Popcorn Chicken

Prep Time: 10 minutes/ Cook Time 8 minutes/ Serves: 3

Ingredients:

- 3 chicken breasts, cut into equal sized cubes
- ½ cup buttermilk
- ¼ cup cornstarch
- 2 cups corn flakes cereal, finely crushed
- ¼ tsp garlic powder
- ¼ tsp onion powder
- ¼ tsp paprika
- Salt and pepper to taste

Directions:

1. Preheat the Ninja Air Fryer to 400 degrees F.
2. Place the buttermilk, corn starch and corn flakes in separate bowls for coating the chicken.
3. Coat each piece of chicken first in corn starch, then in buttermilk and finally in the corn flakes crumbs before placing in the air fryer basket. Cook for 8 minutes. Serve with ketchup or your favorite dipping sauce.

Nutrition value per serving: Calories: 392 kcal, Carbs: 28.2 g, Fat: 10.8 g, Protein: 43.3 g.

Honey BBQ Wings

Prep Time: 15 minutes/ Cook Time 30 minutes/ Serves: 5

Ingredients:

- 10 chicken wing pieces
- 2 tsp honey
- 2 tsp barbecue sauce
- 1 tbsp. soy sauce
- 1 tsp lime juice
- ¼ tsp fresh ginger, finely chopped
- 1 garlic cloves, minced
- ½ tsp cornstarch

- Olive oil
- Salt and pepper to taste

Directions:

1. Preheat the Ninja Air Fryer to 400 degrees F.
2. Coat the chicken wings lightly with the olive oil. Season with salt and pepper.
3. Place the chicken wings in the air fryer basket for 25 minutes or until the outer skin is crisp. Turn the chicken wings halfway through the cooking process.
4. Whisk the cornstarch and soy sauce in a small skillet and place over medium heat on the stovetop. Add in the remaining ingredients and allow this to come to a boil so that the sauce thickens. Cook for 1 minute.
5. Place the cooked chicken wings in a large heat resistant bowl and coat with the honey barbecue sauce. Toss to coat. Serve.

Nutrition value per serving: Calories: 306 kcal, Carbs: 4 g, Fat: 13.2 g, Protein: 40.8 g.

SUCCULENT TURKEY BREAST

Prep Time: 5 minutes/ Cook Time 30 minutes/ Serves: 4

Ingredients:

- 2 lb. turkey breast
- ½ tbsp. all-purpose seasoning
- Olive oil
- Salt and pepper to taste

Directions:

1. Preheat the Ninja Air Fryer to 350 degrees F.
2. Coat the turkey in the olive oil and season with the remaining ingredients.
3. Place the turkey into the air fryer basket skin side down and cook for 30 minutes. Flip half way through. The turkey will have an internal temperature of 160 degrees F when it is done. Allow the turkey to rest for 10 minutes before serving.

Nutrition value per serving: Calories: 266 kcal, Carbs: 9.6 g, Fat: 7.3 g, Protein: 38.7 g.

CHICKEN PARMESAN

Prep Time: 7 minutes/ Cook Time 9 minutes/ Serves: 5

Ingredients:

- 4 thin chicken breast cutlets
- 2 tbsp. Parmesan cheese grated
- 5 tbsp. of seasoned breadcrumbs
- 1 tbsp. olive oil
- ½ cup marinara sauce
- 6 tbsp. mozzarella cheese

Directions:

1. Preheat the Ninja Air Fryer to 360 degrees F.
2. Combine the Parmesan cheese and breadcrumbs in a bowl.
3. Brush the chicken with the olive oil then dip into the bread crumb mixture.
4. Place the chicken breasts into the air fryer basket and cook for 6 minutes.
5. Top each chicken breast piece with marinara sauce and mozzarella cheese. Cook for 3 more minutes or until the cheese has melted.
6. Serve warm.

Nutrition value per serving: Calories: 272 kcal, Carbs: 5.5 g, Fat: 14 g, Protein: 30.7 g.

ROTISSERIE CHICKEN

Prep Time: 15 minutes/ Cook Time 50 minutes/ Serves: 5

Ingredients:

- 1 whole chicken
- 4 cups buttermilk
- Salt and pepper to taste

Directions:

1. Prepare the chicken the night before by seasoning with the salt and pepper. Allow this to sit for no more than an hour.
2. Tie the chicken legs together with butcher's twine then place in a large bowl containing the buttermilk. Seal the bowl and refrigerate the chicken overnight.
3. Remove the chicken from the refrigerator 1 hour before air frying.
4. Preheat the ninja air fryer to 350 degrees F.

5. Remove the chicken from the buttermilk and pat of the excess buttermilk before placing in the air fryer belly side down. Season the top of the chicken with more salt and pepper.
6. Cook for 50 minutes. Flip halfway through when the top of the chicken has browned. Remove from the air fryer when the other side of the chicken has browned and when clear juice runs when a knife has been inserted between the thigh and the leg.
7. Allow the chicken to rest for at least 10 minutes before serving.

Nutrition value per serving: Calories: 134 kcal, Carbs: 9.4 g, Fat: 3.9 g, Protein: 14.9 g.

ASIAN CHICKEN DRUMSTICKS

Prep Time: 15 minutes/ Cook Time 20 minutes/ Serves: 4

Ingredients:

- 8 skinless chicken drumsticks
- 1 tsp sriracha hot sauce
- 3 tbsp. soy sauce
- 2 tbsp. balsamic vinegar
- 1 tbsp. honey
- 1-inch piece fresh ginger, grated
- 3 garlic cloves, crushed

Directions:

1. Combine the soy sauce, balsamic vinegar, garlic, honey, ginger and sriracha sauce in a small bowl. Mix well and pour half of the marinade into a large bowl. Add the chicken. Toss and marinate for at least 2 hours.
2. Preheat the Ninja Air Fryer to 400 degrees F.
3. Remove the chicken from the marinade and place in the air fryer basket. Cook for 14 minutes. Flip the chicken pieces halfway through the cooking process.
4. While the chicken cooks, heat the remaining marinade mixture in a small pot and cook for 2 minutes so that the sauce thickens.
5. Toss the chicken with the sauce. Garnish and serve.

Nutrition value per serving: Calories: 200 kcal, Carbs: 6.3 g, Fat: 7 g, Protein: 26.5 g.

Chicken Cordon Bleu

Prep Time: 15 minutes/ Cook Time 12 minutes/ Serves: 6

Ingredients:

- 6 thin skinless boneless chicken breasts
- 3 slices of deli Ham, each sliced in half
- 3 slices Swiss cheese, each sliced in half
- 2 tbsp. Parmesan cheese grated
- 4 tbsp. panko breadcrumbs
- 1 small egg, beaten
- 2 egg whites, whisked
- ½ tbsp. water
- Olive oil
- Salt and pepper to taste

Directions:

1. Preheat the Ninja Air Fryer to 400 degrees F.
2. Ensure that the chicken pieces have been patted dry. Pound to make finer and season with the salt and pepper.
3. Lay a piece of ham and cheese on top of each chicken piece. Roll and place seam side down.
4. Combine the egg whites, egg and water to make an egg wash in a medium-sized bowl.
5. In another bowl, combine the Parmesan cheese and panko breadcrumbs.
6. Dip each piece of chicken first into the egg wash and then into the bread crumb mixture.
7. Place the chicken seam side down in the air fryer basket and spray with olive oil. Cook for 12 minutes. Flip halfway through the cooking process.
8. Allow to sit for at least 10 minutes before serving.

Nutrition value per serving: Calories: 169 kcal, Carbs: 2.1 g, Fat: 9.4 g, Protein: 19.1 g.

Stuffed Chicken

Prep Time: 15 minutes/ Cook Time 12 minutes/ Serves: 4

Ingredients:

- 4 thin chicken cutlets

- 2 slices of mozzarella cheese, each piece sliced in half
- 2 slices prosciutto, each piece sliced in half
- 4 slices roasted peppers
- 1 cup baby spinach
- ¼ cup seasoned bread crumbs
- 1 tbsp. lemon juice
- 1 tbsp. olive oil
- Salt and pepper to taste

Directions:

1. Preheat the Ninja Air Fryer to 400 degrees F.
2. Ensure that the chicken pieces have been patted dry.
3. Combine the olive oil, lemon juice, salt and pepper in one bowl. Place the breadcrumbs in another bowl.
4. Place one piece of prosciutto cheese, roasted pepper and ¼ of the spinach on one side of the chicken. Roll the chicken and place seam side down.
5. Dip the chicken into the olive oil mixture and then the bread crumbs before placing in the air fryer basket.
6. Air fry for 12 minutes. Flip halfway through the cooking process.
7. Allow to sit for at least 10 minutes before serving.

Nutrition value per serving: Calories: 148 kcal, Carbs: 6.5 g, Fat: 7.4 g, Protein: 14.1 g.

Turkey Burgers

Prep Time: 15 minutes/ Cook Time 10 minutes/ Serves: 4

Ingredients:

- 1 lb. lean ground turkey
- 1/3 cup seasoned bread crumbs
- 1 small red onion, grated
- 1 garlic clove, grated
- Olive oil
- Salt and pepper to taste

Directions:

1. Combine all the ingredients in a large bowl.
2. Divide the mixture into 4 equal parts that are ½" thick.
3. Preheat the Ninja Air Fryer to 370 degrees F.

4. Place the turkey patties in the air fryer basket and cook for 10 minutes. Flip the parties halfway through the cooking process.
5. Remove the cooked patties from the air fryer basket and assemble veggies and hamburger buns to form a turkey burger.

Nutrition value per serving: Calories: 224 kcal, Carbs: 8.8 g, Fat: 10.4 g, Protein: 23.9 g.

HERBED CHICKEN TENDERLOINS

Prep Time: 8 minutes/ Cook Time 12 minutes/ Serves: 4

Ingredients:

- 4 chicken tenderloins
- ¼ cup seasoned breadcrumbs
- 1 tbsp. olive oil
- 1 egg, whisked

Directions:

1. Preheat the Ninja Air Fryer to 350 degrees F.
2. Place the egg in a small bowl. Mix the olive oil and breadcrumbs in another bowl to form a loose and crumbly mixture.
3. First, dip the chicken tenderloins into the egg and then into the breadcrumb mixture. Coat evenly and place in the air fryer basket.
4. Cook the chicken tenderloins for 12 minutes. Flip halfway through the cooking process. Serve warm.

Nutrition value per serving: Calories: 133 kcal, Carbs: 1.1 g, Fat: 5.3 g, Protein: 20.6 g.

WHOLE TURKEY

Prep Time: 15 minutes/ Cook Time 3 hours / Serves: 6

Ingredients:

- 12 lb. whole turkey, giblet package removed
- 4 tbsp. butter, sliced
- 4 garlic cloves, thinly sliced
- Olive oil
- 1 ½ cup vegetable broth
- Salt and pepper to taste

Directions:

1. Preheat the Ninja Air Fryer to 350 degrees F.
2. Pat the turkey dry and stuff the butter slices and garlic between the skin and turkey breast.
3. Combine the olive oil, salt and pepper. Rub the turkey with this mixture.
4. Place the turkey breast side down on the lowest rack of the air fryer.
5. Pour ½ cup of the broth over the turkey and air fry for up to 3 hours.
6. Baste the turkey with the remaining broth every 30 minutes. Flip the turkey 2 hours into the baking process. The turkey is done when it has reached an internal temperature of 165 degrees F at the thickest part of the thigh.
7. Allow the turkey to rest for at least 20 minutes before serving.

Nutrition value per serving: Calories: 124 kcal, Carbs: 1.7 g, Fat: 10.8 g, Protein: 5.4 g.

TURKEY MEATBALLS

Prep Time: 15 minutes/ Cook Time 8 minutes/ Serves: 12

Ingredients:

- 1 lb. ground turkey
- 1 small egg, lightly beaten
- 1 red bell pepper, finely chopped
- 2 tbsp. fresh parsley minced
- Salt and pepper to taste

Directions:

1. Preheat the Ninja Air Fryer to 400 degrees F.
2. Mix all the ingredients in a large bowl and shape into to 1 ¼" meatballs.
3. Place the meatballs in a single layer in the air fryer basket and cook for 8 minutes or until they have become lightly browned. Flip halfway through the cooking process. Serve warm.

Nutrition value per serving: Calories: 83 kcal, Carbs: 0.9 g, Fat: 4.5 g, Protein: 10.9 g.

TURKEY LEGS

Prep Time: 7 minutes/ Cook Time 25 minutes/ Serves: 4

Ingredients:

- 4 turkey legs
- 1 tbsp. olive oil
- ¼ tsp dried rosemary
- ¼ tsp dried oregano
- ¼ tsp thyme
- Salt and pepper to taste

Directions:

1. Preheat the Ninja Air Fryer to 350 degrees F.
2. Combine all the seasonings and olive oil in a small bowl.
3. Rub the turkey legs with the seasoning mixture and place in the air fryer basket. Cook for 25 minutes or until the turkey legs have reached an internal temperature of 165 degrees F.
4. Serve warm.

Nutrition value per serving: Calories: 131 kcal, Carbs: 0.2 g, Fat: 5.7 g, Protein: 19 g.

SIMPLE CHICKEN BREAST

Prep Time: 5 minutes/ Cook Time 15 minutes/ Serves: 4

Ingredients:

- 4 boneless skinless chicken breasts
- ½ tsp garlic powder
- ½ tsp onion powder
- ½ tsp paprika
- 1 tbsp. olive oil
- Salt and pepper to taste

Directions:

1. Preheat the Ninja Air Fryer to 375 degrees F.
2. Combine the seasonings and olive oil in a small.
3. Rub the chicken breast with this seasoned mixture. Coat evenly and place in the air fryer basket.
4. Air Fry for 15 minutes. Flip halfway through the cooking process.
5. Allow the chicken to sit for at least 10 minutes before serving.

Nutrition value per serving: Calories: 63 kcal, Carbs: 0.7 g, Fat: 3.9 g, Protein: 6.6 g.

Breaded Chicken

Prep Time: 15 minutes/ Cook Time 22 minutes/ Serves: 4

Ingredients:

- 4 boneless skinless chicken
- 1 cup seasoned breadcrumbs
- 1 cup all-purpose flour
- 1 egg, whisked
- Salt and pepper to taste

Directions:

1. Preheat the Ninja Air Fryer to 350 degrees F.
2. Combine the flour, salt and pepper in a bowl.
3. Place the egg and breadcrumbs into 2 other bowls.
4. Pound the chicken breasts into thin layers then dip the chicken first into the flour mixture then into the egg and lastly, into the bread crumb mixture. Coat well.
5. Lay the chicken into the air fryer basket and cook for 22 minutes.
6. Serve warm.

Nutrition value per serving: Calories: 187 kcal, Carbs: 28.2 g, Fat: 2.7 g, Protein: 11.9 g.

Chapter 6. Fish and Seafood Recipes

Simple Citrus Salmon

Prep Time: 7 minutes/ Cook Time 8 minutes/ Serves: 4

Ingredients:

- 4 fresh salmon fillets
- 1 large lemon
- ½ tsp paprika
- Salt and pepper to taste

Directions:

1. Preheat the Ninja Air Fryer to 375 degrees F.
2. Season the salmon with all of the spices.
3. Slice lemons thinly and evenly divide the slices by placing them on top of the salmon pieces
4. Place the salmon pieces in an even layer in the air fryer basket and cook for 8 minutes. The salmon is done when it reaches an internal temperature of 145 degrees F at the thickest part of the meat.
5. Garnish as desired and serve.

Nutrition value per serving: Calories: 240 kcal, Carbs: 1.5 g, Fat: 11.1 g, Protein: 34.7 g.

Maple-Flavored Salmon

Prep Time: 15 minutes/ Cook Time 12 minutes/ Serves: 4

Ingredients:

- 4 fresh salmon fillets
- 2 tbsp. of maple syrup
- 3 tbsp. soy sauce
- 1 tbsp. sriracha hot sauce
- 1 garlic clove, minced

Directions:

1. Combine all ingredients in a sealable plastic bag. Allow the salmon to marinate for at least 30 minutes.
2. Preheat the Ninja Air Fryer to 400 degrees F.

3. Remove the salmon from the marinade and pat dry before placing in the air fryer basket. Cook for 8 minutes.
4. While the salmon cooks, place the marinade into a small saucepan over medium heat on the stove top. Cook for 1-2 minutes to reduce the sauce.
5. Glaze the sauce over the salmon pieces and serve.

Nutrition value per serving: Calories: 269 kcal, Carbs: 7.9 g, Fat: 11 g, Protein: 35.3 g.

CAJUN SHRIMP

Prep Time: 5 minutes/ Cook Time 8 minutes/ Serves: 5

Ingredients:

- 1 lb. jumbo shrimp, cleaned and peeled
- 1 tbsp. Cajun seasoning
- 1 red bell pepper, sliced
- 1 tbsp. olive oil

Directions:

1. Preheat the Ninja Air Fryer to 400 degrees F.
2. Combine all the ingredients in a large bowl and toss so that the shrimp is thoroughly coated in the seasoning.
3. Transfer the mixture to the air fryer basket and cook for 8 minutes. Stir the basket three times.
4. Serve with desired sides.

Nutrition value per serving: Calories: 96 kcal, Carbs: 1.8 g, Fat: 2.9 g, Protein: 16.5 g.

COCONUT SHRIMP

Prep Time: 10 minutes/ Cook Time 6 minutes/ Serves: 5

Ingredients:

- 1 lb. jumbo shrimp, cleaned and peeled
- ½ cup unsweetened coconut
- ½ cup all-purpose flour
- ¼ cup seasoned breadcrumbs
- 2 eggs, beaten
- Salt and pepper to taste

Directions:

1. Preheat the Ninja Air Fryer to 400 degrees F.
2. Place the eggs in a shallow, wide bowl. Combine the breadcrumbs, coconut and spices in a separate bowl.
3. Dredge the shrimp in first, the egg, and then the breadcrumb mixture to coat thoroughly.
4. Place the shrimp in the air fryer basket in a single layer and cook for 5 minutes. Stir at least twice.
5. Serve warm.

Nutrition value per serving: Calories: 169 kcal, Carbs: 11.8 g, Fat: 4.7 g, Protein: 20.1 g.

BREADED CATFISH

Prep Time: 8 minutes/ Cook Time 8 minutes/ Serves: 5

Ingredients:

- 4 catfish fillets
- ½ cup seasoned breadcrumbs
- ½ cup all-purpose flour
- 1 egg, beaten
- Salt and pepper to taste

Directions:

1. Preheat the Ninja Air Fryer 400 degrees F.
2. Toss the catfish with flour to coat.
3. Coat in the beaten egg.
4. Dredge in the breadcrumbs.
5. Place in the air fryer basket and air fry for 8 minutes.
6. Sprinkle with salt and pepper and serve.

Nutrition value per serving: Calories: 344 kcal, Carbs: 20.5 g, Fat: 15.1 g, Protein: 29.4 g.

RANCH COD FILLET

Prep Time: 8 minutes/ Cook Time 12 minutes/ Serves: 4

Ingredients:

- 4 cod fillets

- ½ cup panko bread crumbs
- 1 packet dry ranch seasoning mix
- 2 eggs, beaten
- 2 tbsp. olive oil

Directions:

1. Preheat the Ninja Air Fryer to 400 degrees F.
2. Mix the olive oil, breadcrumbs and ranch seasoning mix until a loose and crumbly mixture is formed.
3. Dip the cod fillets into the egg and then into the bread crumb mixture to coat thoroughly.
4. Place the cod fillets into the air fryer basket and cook for 12 minutes.
5. Garnish and serve.

Nutrition value per serving: Calories: 236 kcal, Carbs: 9.9 g, Fat: 10.9 g, Protein: 24.6 g.

BACON-WRAPPED SCALLIONS

Prep Time: 9 minutes/ Cook Time 8 minutes/ Serves: 4

Ingredients:

- 8 large scallops, cleaned
- 4 pieces bacon, cut down the center lengthwise
- Olive oil
- Salt and pepper to taste

Directions:

1. Preheat the Ninja Air Fryer to 400 degrees F.
2. Remove any side muscles from the scallops and pat dry with paper towels.
3. Wrap each scallop in a piece of bacon and secure with a toothpick.
4. Coat the scallops with olive oil then season with salt and pepper.
5. Place the scallops in a single layer in the air fryer basket and cook for 8 minutes. Flip halfway through the cooking process.
6. Serve warm.

Nutrition value per serving: Calories: 171 kcal, Carbs: 1.7 g, Fat: 10.2 g, Protein: 17.1 g.

AIR FRYER OYSTERS

Prep Time: 9 minutes/ Cook Time 2 minutes/ Serves: 3

Ingredients:

- 12 fresh oysters, shucked
- 2 large eggs, beaten
- 1 cup seasoned breadcrumbs
- ½ cup all-purpose flour
- Olive oil
- Salt and pepper to taste

Directions:

1. Preheat the Ninja Air Fryer to 400 degrees F.
2. Place the beaten egg in one bowl, the flour in another and finally, the bread crumbs in a shallow bowl.
3. Bread the oysters by first dipping them into the flour then the egg and finally, the breadcrumbs.
4. Line the oysters in a single layer in the air fryer basket. Spray with olive oil. Cook for 2 minutes. Stir the oysters at the 1 minute mark.
5. Sprinkle with salt and pepper and serve.

Nutrition value per serving: Calories: 377 kcal, Carbs: 41.5 g, Fat: 15.2 g, Protein: 17 g.

FRENCH MUSSELS

Prep Time: 5 minutes/ Cook Time 10 minutes/ Serves: 4

Ingredients:

- 1 lb. mussels
- ¼ cup dry white wine
- 2 tbsp. low fat butter
- 2 tbsp. coconut cream
- 4 garlic cloves, minced
- Salt and pepper to taste

Directions:

1. Preheat the Ninja Air Fryer to 400 degrees F.
2. Mix all the ingredients together in a large bowl.
3. Cook in the air fryer for 10 minutes. Shake the basket halfway through the

cooking process.

4. Plate and serve.

Nutrition value per serving: Calories: 197 kcal, Carbs: 13.5 g, Fat: 5.7 g, Protein: 19.4 g.

AIR FRYER CLAMS

Prep Time: 2 minutes/ Cook Time 13 minutes/ Serves: 5

Ingredients:

- 1 lb. frozen clam strips
- Olive oil
- Salt and pepper to taste

Directions:

1. Preheat the Ninja Air Fryer to 400 degrees F.
2. Place the frozen clams into the air fryer basket and spray with olive oil. Cook for 13 minutes. Shake the basket halfway through the cooking process.
3. Sprinkle with salt and pepper and serve.

Nutrition value per serving: Calories: 78 kcal, Carbs: 2.6 g, Fat: 6 g, Protein: 3.4 g.

CRAB CAKES

Prep Time: 5 minutes/ Cook Time 10 minutes/ Serves: 5

Ingredients:

- 8 oz. crab meat
- 1 tbsp. Dijon mustard
- 2 tbsp. mayonnaise
- 2 tbsp. seasoned breadcrumbs
- 1 tsp all-purpose seasoning
- 1 small yellow onion, diced
- 1/3 cup bell pepper, finely chopped
- Olive oil

Directions:

1. Preheat the Ninja Air Fryer to 370 degrees F.
2. Combine all the ingredients except for the olive oil in a bowl. Form 4

large parties or 5 small parties with the mixture.

3. Place the patties in the air fryer basket and lightly spray with the olive oil. Cook for 10 minutes. Serve warm.

Nutrition value per serving: Calories: 109 kcal, Carbs: 6 g, Fat: 6.1 g, Protein: 6.4 g.

AHI TUNA STEAKS

Prep Time: 7 minutes/ Cook Time 10 minutes/ Serves: 4

Ingredients:

- 4 tuna steaks
- 2 egg white, beaten
- 1/2 cup sesame seeds
- Salt and pepper to taste

Directions:

1. Preheat the Ninja Air Fryer to 400 degrees F.
2. Dip the tuna steaks into the egg whites then coat with the sesame seeds, salt and pepper.
3. Place in the air fryer basket and cook for 8 minutes. Flip halfway through the cooking process.
4. Garnish and serve.

Nutrition value per serving: Calories: 268 kcal, Carbs: 4.4 g, Fat: 14.3 g, Protein: 30.4 g.

TUNA PATTIES

Prep Time: 15 minutes/ Cook Time 10 minutes/ Serves: 5

Ingredients:

- ½ lb. of canned tuna
- 1 large egg, beaten
- 1 cup breadcrumbs
- 1 tbsp. Parmesan cheese grated
- 2 tsp lemon juice
- Zest of 1 small lemon
- ¼ tsp garlic powder
- ¼ tsp dried oregano

- ½ yellow onion, minced
- ¼ cup fresh parsley, finely chopped
- Olive oil spray
- Salt and pepper to taste

Directions:

1. Preheat the Ninja Air Fryer to 360 degrees F.
2. Combine all the ingredients in a large bowl until just mixed. Form 3" wide and ½" thick parties and lay in the air fryer basket.
3. Brush the patties with olive oil and cook for 10 minutes. Flip halfway through the cooking process.
4. Garnish and serve with your favorite sauce.

Nutrition value per serving: Calories: 196 kcal, Carbs: 17.2 g, Fat: 6.3 g, Protein: 16.9 g.

SIMPLE COD

Prep Time: 3 minutes/ Cook Time 10 minutes/ Serves: 2

Ingredients:

- 2 cod fillets
- Olive oil
- Salt and pepper to taste

Directions:

1. Preheat the Ninja Air Fryer to 400 degrees F.
2. Season the cod with the salt and pepper.
3. Place the seasoned cod in the air fryer basket and spray with olive oil. Cook for 10 minutes. Flip halfway through the cooking process.
4. Serve warm.

Nutrition value per serving: Calories: 120 kcal, Carbs: 0 g, Fat: 4.5 g, Protein: 20 g.

LOBSTER TAILS

Prep Time: 15 minutes/ Cook Time 7 minutes/ Serves: 2

Ingredients:

- 1 lobster tail
- 2 tbsp. butter

- 1 garlic clove, grated
- 1 tsp lemon zest
- Salt and pepper to taste

Directions:

1. Butterfly the lobster tail lengthwise and spread the halves apart.
2. Add the butter, garlic and lemon zest to a small saucepan and place over medium heat on the stove top. Melt the butter and cook for about 30 seconds so that the garlic becomes tender.
3. Brush the butter mixture answer the lobster tail then season with salt and pepper.
4. Preheat the Ninja Air Fryer to 390 degrees F.
5. Place the lobster tail meat side up in the air fryer and cook for 7 minutes.
6. Brush the lobster meat with any remaining sauce and garnish as desired. Serve.

Nutrition value per serving: Calories: 143 kcal, Carbs: 0.8 g, Fat: 11.9 g, Protein: 8.3 g.

Chapter 7. Vegan and Vegetarian Recipes

Tempeh Bacon

Prep Time: 25 minutes/ Cook Time 10 minutes/ Serves: 4

Ingredients:

- 4 oz. tempeh, thinly sliced
- 1 tbsp. maple syrup
- ½ tsp garlic powder
- ¼ tsp black pepper
- ¼ cup soy sauce

Directions:

1. Mix all the ingredients in a shallow bowl so that the tempeh slices marinade. Allowed to sit for 10 minutes.
2. Preheat the Ninja Air Fryer to 350 degrees F.
3. Place a piece of parchment paper at the bottom of the air fryer basket and layer the tempeh pieces in an even layer on it.
4. Cook the slices for 10 minutes. Flip halfway through the cooking process.
5. Use these bacon slices just as you would use any other type of bacon slices.

Nutrition value per serving: Calories: 78 kcal, Carbs: 7.6 g, Fat: 3.1 g, Protein: 6.3 g.

Vegetarian Breakfast Casserole

Prep Time: 15 minutes/ Cook Time 30 minutes/ Serves: 3

Ingredients:

- 6 eggs
- ¼ cup almond milk
- 2 oz. ricotta cheese
- 4 oz. mushrooms, quartered and roasted
- 1 cup broccoli florets, roasted
- 1 small yellow onion diced, roasted

- ¼ cup red bell pepper, roasted
- 1 garlic cloves, minced
- 2 tbsp. fresh parsley, chopped
- 1 tsp dried oregano
- 1 tbsp. olive oil
- Salt and pepper to taste

Directions:

1. Preheat the Ninja Air Fryer to 400 degrees F and spray a small baking dish with non-stick spray.
2. Line the bottom of the prepared baking sheet with the vegetables.
3. Mix the eggs, milk, garlic and other seasonings in a large bowl and pour over the prepared vegetables.
4. Dollop the ricotta cheese in small spoonfuls over the prepared dish.
5. Place the baking dish in the air fryer and cook for 30 minutes or until the top of the casserole is golden brown and the center no longer jiggles.
6. Garnish as desired and serve warm.

Nutrition value per serving: Calories: 279 kcal, Carbs: 11.6 g, Fat: 20 g, Protein: 16.4 g.

SCRAMBLED TOFU

Prep Time: 15 minutes/ Cook Time 50 minutes/ Serves: 3

Ingredients:

- 1 block tofu, drained and chopped into 1-inch pieces
- 1 tbsp. olive oil
- 1 tsp soy sauce
- 1 tsp turmeric
- 1 tsp garlic powder
- 1 tsp onion powder

Directions:

1. Add all the ingredients to a medium-sized bowl and mix well so that the tofu marinates. Set aside for at least 10 minutes.
2. Preheat the Ninja Air Fryer to 370 degrees F.
3. Remove the tofu from the marinate and air fry for 15 minutes. Shake the air fryer basket halfway through the cooking process.
4. Plate and serve as you would scrambled eggs.

Nutrition value per serving: Calories: 71 kcal, Carbs: 2.4 g, Fat: 6 g, Protein: 2.9 g.

Buffalo Cauliflower

Prep Time: 10 minutes/ Cook Time 20 minutes/ Serves: 5

Ingredients:

- 4 cups cauliflower florets
- 1 cup all-purpose flour
- 1 tsp all-purpose seasoning
- ¼ tsp chili powder
- ¼ tsp cayenne pepper
- 1 cup soy milk
- 2 tbsp. vegan butter
- 1/3 cup hot sauce
- 2 garlic cloves, minced

Directions:

1. Preheat the Ninja Air Fryer to 390 degrees F.
2. Combine the seasonings and flour in a large bowl. Whisk in the milk to form a thick batter.
3. Toss the cauliflower florets in the batter and transfer to the air fryer basket. Cook for 20 minutes. Flip the cauliflower halfway through the cooking process.
4. While the cauliflower cooks, place the butter, hot sauce and garlic in a small saucepan over medium heat on a stove top. Bring to a boil then simmer for 5 minutes on low heat.
5. Once the cauliflower has cooked, transfer to a large bowl and pour the hot sauce mixture over. Gently toss and serve immediately.

Nutrition value per serving: Calories: 151 kcal, Carbs: 27.5 g, Fat: 2.2 g, Protein: 6 g.

Roasted Cauliflower

Prep Time: 3 minutes/ Cook Time 15 minutes/ Serves: 4

Ingredients:

- 4 cups cauliflower florets
- 3 garlic cloves, minced

- 1 tbsp. olive oil
- Salt and pepper to taste

Directions:

1. Preheat the Ninja Air Fryer to 400 degrees F.
2. Mix all the ingredients then place the seasoned cauliflower in the air fryer basket. Cook for 15 minutes. Shake the basket every few minutes.
3. Serve warm.

Nutrition value per serving: Calories: 58 kcal, Carbs: 6.1 g, Fat: 3.6 g, Protein: 2.1 g.

BBQ RANCH CHICKPEAS

Prep Time: 2 minutes/ Cook Time 12 minutes/ Serves: 4

Ingredients:

- 1 can chickpeas, drained and rinsed
- 1 tsp dry ranch seasoning mix
- 2 tbsp. BBQ sauce

Directions:

1. Preheat the Ninja Air Fryer to 350 degrees F.
2. Mix all the ingredients in a bowl and place the chicken in the air fryer. Cook for 12 minutes. Shake the basket halfway through the cooking process.
3. Allow to cool and serve.

Nutrition value per serving: Calories: 195 kcal, Carbs: 33.2 g, Fat: 3 g, Protein: 9.7 g.

CORN ON THE COB

Prep Time: 2 minutes/ Cook Time 8 minutes/ Serves: 2

Ingredients:

- 2 ears sweet corn, halved
- 1 tbsp. olive oil
- Salt and pepper to taste

Directions:

1. Preheat the Ninja Air Fryer to 380 degrees F.
2. Rub the corn with the olive oil then place in the air fryer basket. Cook for 8 minutes. Shake the basket halfway through the cooking process.
3. Sprinkle with salt and pepper and serve.

Nutrition value per serving: Calories: 192 kcal, Carbs: 29 g, Fat: 8.8 g, Protein: 5 g.

EASY FRENCH TOAST

Prep Time: 3 minutes/ Cook Time 4 minutes/ Serves: 1

Ingredients:

- 2 slices almond bread
- ½ cup coconut milk
- 1 tsp baking powder

Directions:

1. Preheat the Ninja Air Fryer to 350 degrees F.
2. Mix the coconut milk and baking powder in a shallow wide bowl.
3. Dip each slice of bread into the coconut milk mixture and place into the air fryer basket. Cook for 4 minutes then top with your favorite sauce or toppings and serve.

Nutrition value per serving: Calories: 148 kcal, Carbs: 5.9 g, Fat: 14.5 g, Protein: 1.5 g.

POTATO CHIPS

Prep Time: 5 minutes/ Cook Time 15 minutes/ Serves: 2

Ingredients:

- 1 large russet potato, thinly sliced
- Olive oil spray
- Salt to taste

Directions:

1. Preheat the Ninja Air Fryer to 400 degrees F.
2. Blot the potato slices with paper towel to ensure that they are as dry as possible then spray with olive oil and sprinkle with salt.
3. Air fry potato chips for 15 minutes or until golden brown. Shake the basket halfway through the cooking process.

4. Serve.

Nutrition value per serving: Calories: 148 kcal, Carbs: 33.3 g, Fat: 0.4 g, Protein: 4 g.

SPINACH POTATO NUGGETS

Prep Time: 15 minutes/ Cook Time 15 minutes/ Serves: 2

Ingredients:

- 1 cup potatoes, mashed
- 2 cups spinach, chopped
- ½ tsp olive oil
- 1 tbsp. almond milk
- 1 garlic clove, minced
- Salt and pepper to taste

Directions:

1. Heat the olive oil in a large skillet over medium heat on the stove top.
2. Sauté the garlic and spinach for 3 minutes.
3. Mix the milk, potatoes, salt and pepper then combine with the cooked spinach.
4. Preheat the Ninja Air Fryer to 390 degrees F.
5. Roll the potato spinach mixture into 1" nuggets and spray with olive oil spray then air fry for 15 minutes or until golden brown. Shake the basket halfway through the cooking process.
6. Serve with your favorite dipping sauce.

Nutrition value per serving: Calories: 88 kcal, Carbs: 13.8 g, Fat: 3.2 g, Protein: 2.4 g.

VEGETARIAN CORN FRITTERS

Prep Time: 5 minutes/ Cook Time 8 minutes/ Serves: 4

Ingredients:

- 2 cups corn
- 1/3 cup all-purpose flour
- 1 small egg
- ½ tsp cumin
- 1 scallion, thinly sliced

- Olive oil spray
- Salt and pepper to taste

Directions:

1. Preheat the Ninja Air Fryer to 390 degrees F.
2. Combine all the ingredients in a large bowl. Add 1-2 tablespoons of water if the batter is too thick.
3. Line the bottom of the air fryer basket with parchment paper and place spoonfuls of the corn fritter batter on it. Air fry for 8 minutes until golden brown. Flip halfway through cooking process.
4. Serve with your favorite dipping sauce.

Nutrition value per serving: Calories: 121 kcal, Carbs: 22.9 g, Fat: 2.1 g, Protein: 4.9 g.

ITALIAN-FLAVORED TOFU

Prep Time: 15 minutes/ Cook Time 6 minutes/ Serves: 5

Ingredients:

- 1 block tofu, cut into 1" squares
- 1 tbsp. of soy sauce
- 1tbsp vegetable broth
- 1 tbsp. of dry Italian seasoning
- Black pepper to taste

Directions:

1. Combine all the ingredients in a sealable plastic bag and allowed to marinate for at least 10 minutes.
2. Preheat the Ninja Air Fryer to 390 degrees F.
3. Remove the tofu from the bag and blot dry before arranging in a single layer in the air fryer basket.
4. Air fry for 6 minutes. Flip halfway through the cooking process.
5. Serve with vegan or vegetarian friendly Italian sauce.

Nutrition value per serving: Calories: 24 kcal, Carbs: 0.9 g, Fat: 1.6 g, Protein: 1.8 g.

BRUSSEL SPROUT CHIPS

Prep Time: 4 minutes/ Cook Time 12 minutes/ Serves: 5

Ingredients:

- ½ lb. Brussel sprouts, rinsed and dried
- 1 tbsp. olive oil
- Salt and pepper to taste

Directions:

1. Preheat the Ninja Air Fryer to 360 degrees F.
2. Toss the Brussel sprouts with the rest of the ingredients then transfer to the air fryer basket and cook for 12 minutes or until slightly brown. Shake the basket halfway through the cooking process.
3. Serve.

Nutrition value per serving: Calories: 44 kcal, Carbs: 4.1 g, Fat: 3 g, Protein: 1.6 g.

VEGETARIAN BLOOMING ONION

Prep Time: 5 minutes/ Cook Time 370 minutes/ Serves: 2

Ingredients:

- 1 large sweet onions
- 1 tbsp. all-purpose seasoning
- ½ cup all-purpose flour
- ¼ cup almond milk
- 1 tsp garlic powder
- ½ tsp cayenne pepper
- 1 egg

Directions:

1. Preheat the Ninja Air Fryer to 370 degrees F.
2. Cut the onions into sections so that it resembles a blooming flower.
3. Combine the flour and spices in a medium bowl and the egg and milk in another bowl.
4. Dip the onion into the egg mixture cut side down. Use a spoon to pour the liquid over the onion that it is thoroughly coated.
5. Dip the onion into the flour mixture. Use your hands to sprinkle flour so that the entire onion is coated.
6. Shake off any excess flour and place the onion into the air fryer basket and cook for 10 minutes or until golden brown.

Nutrition value per serving: Calories: 250 kcal, Carbs: 34 g, Fat: 9.8 g, Protein: 7.8 g.

Air Fryer Broccoli

Prep Time: 2 minutes/ Cook Time 5 minutes/ Serves: 2

Ingredients:

- 2 cups broccoli florets
- 1 tbsp. olive oil
- ½ tbsp. nutritional yeast
- Salt and pepper to taste

Directions:

1. Preheat the Ninja Air Fryer to 370 degrees F.
2. Toss all the ingredients together then layer the broccoli into the air fryer basket in a single layer. Cook for 5 minutes. Shake the basket halfway through.
3. Serve with your favorite dipping sauce.

Nutrition value per serving: Calories: 100 kcal, Carbs: 7.2 g, Fat: 7.4 g, Protein: 3.7 g.

CHAPTER 8. APPETIZER RECIPES

AIR FRIED DILL PICKLES

Prep Time: 9 minutes/ Cook Time 16 minutes/ Serves: 2

Ingredients:

- 16 oz. large whole dill pickles, sliced diagonally into ¼" thick slices
- 1 egg
- ¼ cup panko breadcrumbs
- 2 tbsp. Parmesan cheese, grated
- 2 tbsp. dried dill weed

Directions:

1. Preheat the Ninja Air Fryer to 380 degrees F.
2. Combine the breadcrumbs, cheese and dill weed into a shallow bowl and place the egg into another shallow bowl.
3. Dip the pickles into first the egg then the breadcrumb mixture then air fry for 9 minutes.
4. Serve with your favorite dipping sauce.

Nutrition value per serving: Calories: 111 kcal, Carbs: 12.1 g, Fat: 3.9 g, Protein: 5.9 g.

GOAT CHEESE BALLS

Prep Time: 5 minutes/ Cook Time 7 minutes/ Serves: 8

Ingredients:

- 8 oz. soft goat cheese, divided into 24 balls and frozen for a minimum of 30 minutes
- 2 tbsp. all-purpose flour
- ½ cup seasoned breadcrumbs
- 1 egg
- ¼ cup honey

Directions:

1. Preheat the Ninja Air Fryer to 390 degrees F.
2. Place the flour, egg and breadcrumbs into three separate bowls then dip each cheese ball in first the flour then the egg and finally, the

breadcrumbs.

3. Air fry the cheese balls for 7 minutes or until golden brown.
4. Drizzle with honey and serve.

Nutrition value per serving: Calories: 130 kcal, Carbs: 11.6 g, Fat: 6.8 g, Protein: 6.4 g.

EGG ROLLS

Prep Time: 25 minutes/ Cook Time 15 minutes/ Serves: 10

Ingredients:

- 1 pack egg roll wrappers
- 1 lb. ground chicken
- 1 tbsp. olive oil
- 1 tsp ginger, minced
- 1/3 cup green onions, sliced
- 1 tbsp. oyster sauce
- ¼ tsp salt
- 2 cups coleslaw mix

Directions:

1. Heat the olive oil in a large skillet over medium heat on a stove top then cook the onions and Ginger for 1-minute.
2. Add the chicken and season with the salt. Cook until the chicken has browned.
3. Add the coleslaw mix and cook until the cabbage becomes soft.
4. Stir in the oyster sauce and remove the mixture from the heat.
5. Place a small bowl of water next to your work surface and place 2-3 egg roll wrappers there so that the diagonal point is facing you. Place the chicken mixture onto 1/3 of the egg roll wrapper and fold the sides like an envelope. Dip your finger into the water and wet the corners to seal the egg roll.
6. Preheat the Ninja Air Fryer to 390 degrees F then cook the egg rolls for 8 minutes. Flip halfway through the cooking process.
7. Serve.

Nutrition value per serving: Calories: 132 kcal, Carbs: 6.2 g, Fat: 5.5 g, Protein: 14 g.

EGGPLANT FRIES

Prep Time: 10 minutes/ Cook Time 12 minutes/ Serves: 3

Ingredients:

- 1 small eggplant, trimmed and cut into 1/2 inch thick fries
- 2 small eggs, beaten
- ¼ cup Parmesan cheese, grated
- 1 tsp Italian seasoning
- ½ cup toasted wheat germ

Directions:

1. Preheat the Ninja Air Fryer to 400 degrees F.
2. Add the egg to one shallow bowl and combine the cheese, germ wheat and seasoning in another.
3. Dip the eggplant slices into first the egg and then into the cheese mixture.
4. Air fry for 12 minutes. Flip halfway through the cooking process.
5. Serve.

Nutrition value per serving: Calories: 158 kcal, Carbs: 18.8 g, Fat: 5.7 g, Protein: 10.8 g.

TAQUITOS

Prep Time: 10 minutes/ Cook Time 12 minutes/ Serves: 5

Ingredients:

- 5 corn tortillas
- 1 large egg
- 1 tbsp. taco seasoning
- ½ lb. ground beef
- ½ cup bread crumbs
- Olive oil spray

Directions:

1. Preheat the Ninja Air Fryer to 350 degrees F.
2. Combine the eggs, breadcrumbs, taco seasoning and beef in a large bowl.
3. Equally divide the beef mixture and place into the center of each tortilla.
4. Roll the tortillas and secure with a toothpick.
5. Arrange the taquitos into a single layer in the air fryer basket. Spray with

olive oil and cook for 12 minutes. Turn halfway through the cooking process.

6. Serve with salsa or guacamole.

Nutrition value per serving: Calories: 199 kcal, Carbs: 19.2 g, Fat: 5.2 g, Protein: 17.8 g.

ZUCCHINI FRIES

Prep Time: 10 minutes/ Cook Time 7 minutes/ Serves: 3

Ingredients:

- 1 zucchini, cut into 1/2 inch thick fries
- ¼ cup Parmesan cheese, grated
- ¼ cup all-purpose flour
- 1 egg, beaten
- ½ cup panko bread crumbs
- Black pepper to taste

Directions:

1. Preheat the Ninja Air Fryer to 390 degrees F.
2. Place the egg, flour and breadcrumbs into three separate shallow bowls.
3. Dredge the zucchini in first the flour, then in the eggs and finally, the bread crumb mixture.
4. Air fry the zucchini in a single layer for 7 minutes. Shake the basket halfway through the cooking process.
5. Serve with your favorite dipping sauce.

Nutrition value per serving: Calories: 148 kcal, Carbs: 23.3 g, Fat: 3.1 g, Protein: 6.9 g.

TORTILLA CHIPS

Prep Time: 15 minutes/ Cook Time 50 minutes/ Serves: 5

Ingredients:

- 4 corn tortillas
- ½ tbsp. olive oil
- Salt to taste

Directions:

1. Preheat the Ninja Air Fryer to 400 degrees F.
2. Slice the tortillas into triangles and brush with olive oil.
3. Air fry for 3 minutes and sprinkle with salt to serve.

Nutrition value per serving: Calories: 54 kcal, Carbs: 8.6 g, Fat: 2 g, Protein: 1.1 g.

AIR FRIED ASPARAGUS

Prep Time: 5 minutes/ Cook Time 7 minutes/ Serves: 3

Ingredients:

- 1 bunch of asparagus, stems removed, rinsed and dried
- Salt to taste
- 1 tbsp. olive oil

Directions:

1. Preheat the Ninja Air Fryer to 400 degrees F.
2. Toss the asparagus with the salt and olive oil.
3. Air fry for 7 minutes.

Nutrition value per serving: Calories: 41 kcal, Carbs: 0.2 g, Fat: 4.7 g, Protein: 0.1 g.

GINGER SESAME CARROTS

Prep Time: 5 minutes/ Cook Time 7 minutes/ Serves: 2

Ingredients:

- 2 large carrots, sliced
- 2 tbsp. sesame oil
- 1 tbsp. ginger, minced
- 1 tbsp. garlic, minced
- 1 tbsp. soy sauce

Directions:

1. Preheat the Ninja Air Fryer to 375 degrees F.
2. Toss all the ingredients together then arrange in the air fryer basket and cook for 7 minutes. Shake the basket halfway through the cooking process.
3. Garnish and serve.

Nutrition value per serving: Calories: 170 kcal, Carbs: 11 g, Fat: 13.8 g, Protein: 1.6 g.

JALAPENO POPPERS

Prep Time: 15 minutes/ Cook Time 7 minutes/ Serves: 2

Ingredients:

- 5 jalapeno peppers sliced, lengthwise and deseeded
- 5 slices bacon, cut in half lengthwise
- ½ cup Monterey Jack cheese
- 4 oz. cream cheese at room temperature

Directions:

1. Preheat the Ninja Air Fryer to 370 degrees F.
2. Mix the cream cheese and cheese in a bowl then spoon the cheese mixture into the jalapeno halves.
3. Wrap each jalapeno in a slice of bacon and secure with a toothpick.
4. Air fry for 7 minutes or until the tops are golden brown.
5. Serve with your favorite dipping sauce.

Nutrition value per serving: Calories: 221 kcal, Carbs: 3.3 g, Fat: 18 g, Protein: 12 g.

STUFFED MUSHROOMS

Prep Time: 15 minutes/ Cook Time 15 minutes/ Serves: 3

Ingredients:

- 6 mushrooms, stems diced
- ¼ cup cheddar cheese, shredded
- 2 tbsp. sour cream
- 1 slice bacon, diced
- 1 small onion, diced
- 2 tbsp. red bell pepper, diced
- 1 tbsp. olive oil

Directions:

1. Heat the olive oil on the stove top over medium heat and sauté the mushrooms stems, bell peppers, onions and bacon for about 5 minutes. Stir in the sour cream and cheddar cheese. Cook until the cheese has

melted
2. Preheat the Ninja Air Fryer to 350 degrees F.
3. Add the stuffing to the mushroom caps and air fry for 8 minutes.
4. Serve.

Nutrition value per serving: Calories: 172 kcal, Carbs: 9.9 g, Fat: 12.4 g, Protein: 7.1 g.

AIR FRIED BLACK EYED PEAS

Prep Time: 5 minutes/ Cook Time 10 minutes/ Serves: 2

Ingredients:

- 1 can black eyed peas, drained and rinsed
- ½ tsp chili powder
- Salt and pepper to taste

Directions:

1. Preheat the Ninja Air Fryer to 350 degrees F.
2. Mix the seasoning with the black eyed peas and air fry for 10 minutes. Shake the basket halfway through the cooking process.

Nutrition value per serving: Calories: 47 kcal, Carbs: 11.9 g, Fat: 0.1 g, Protein: 4.6 g.

MOZZARELLA STICKS

Prep Time: 2 hours 15 minutes/ Cook Time 7 minutes/ Serves: 4

Ingredients:

- 8 low fat mozzarella sticks
- 1 cup seasoned breadcrumbs
- 1 egg, beaten
- Salt to taste

Directions:

1. Place the egg and bread crumbs into separate bowls. Dip the mozzarella sticks into the egg and then the bread crumbs. Freeze for 1 hour. Repeat this process once more.
2. Preheat the Ninja Air Fryer to 390 degrees F and air fry the mozzarella sticks for 7 minutes or until golden brown and crispy.

Nutrition value per serving: Calories: 203 kcal, Carbs: 6.3 g, Fat: 12 g, Protein: 18.1 g.

POTATO SKINS

Prep Time: 15 minutes/ Cook Time 6 minutes/ Serves: 5

Ingredients:

- 5 small baked potatoes
- ½ cup bacon, crumbled
- ½ cup cheddar cheese, shredded
- ¼ cup fresh parsley, chopped

Directions:

1. Preheat the Ninja Air Fry to 380 degrees F.
2. Slice each potato in half and scoop out the flesh. Ensure that a slight amount of flesh remains on the edges of the potato.
3. Mash the potato flesh and mix with the remaining ingredients. Equally divide and scoop into the potato skins.
4. Air fry for 6 minutes or until the cheese has melted.
5. Serve with your favorite sauce.

Nutrition value per serving: Calories: 185 kcal, Carbs: 30.8 g, Fat: 4.8 g, Protein: 7.1 g.

MAC AND CHEESE BALLS

Prep Time: 1 hour 15 minutes/ Cook Time 10 minutes/ Serves: 4

Ingredients:

- 2 cups cooked macaroni and cheese, chilled
- 1 cup seasoned breadcrumbs
- 1 small egg
- ½ tbsp. almond milk

Directions:

1. Shape the chilled macaroni and cheese into small bite-size balls and freeze overnight.
2. Mix the egg and milk in one bowl and place the breadcrumbs in another.
3. Deep the macaroni and cheese balls first into the egg wash and then into the breadcrumbs then freeze for 1 hour.

4. Preheat the ninja air fryer to 390 degrees F.
5. Air fry for 10 minutes or until the balls are golden brown.
6. Serve with your favorite dipping sauce.

Nutrition value per serving: Calories: 71 kcal, Carbs: 8.1 g, Fat: 3 g, Protein: 3 g.

Chapter 9. Desserts and Snacks

Popcorn

Prep Time: 1 minutes/ Cook Time 15 minutes/ Serves: 5

Ingredients:

- 3 tbsp. corn kernels
- Peanut oil spray
- Salt to taste

Directions:

1. Preheat the Ninja Air Fryer to 390 degrees F.
2. Spray the air fryer basket with the peanut oil.
3. Line the top of the air fryer basket with aluminum foil to prevent the popcorn from flying around in the air fryer and leaving the basket.
4. Air fry for 15 minutes. Check the popcorn every 5 minutes to ensure that the kernels are not burning.
5. Remove the popcorn from the air fryer basket when the popping stops and place in a large bowl. Spray lightly with more peanut oil and sprinkle with salt.

Nutrition value per serving: Calories: 80 kcal, Carbs: 17.4 g, Fat: 1.2 g, Protein: 3 g.

Air Fryer Brownies

Prep Time: 15 minutes/ Cook Time 16 minutes/ Serves: 5

Ingredients:

- ¼ cup cocoa powder
- ½ cup granulated sugar
- ¼ cup all-purpose flour
- ¼ cup butter, melted
- 1 large egg
- ¼ tsp baking powder
- A pinch of salt

Directions:

1. Preheat the Ninja Air Fryer to 350 degrees F and spray a 6" round cake

pan with non-stick spray.
2. Combine the dry ingredients in a large bowl.
3. Whisk together the butter and egg and add the mixture to the dry ingredients. Stir to combine.
4. Transfer the brownie batter to the prepared cake pan. Air fry for 16 minutes.
5. Allow to cool for at least 10 minutes before serving.

Nutrition value per serving: Calories: 203 kcal, Carbs: 27.3 g, Fat: 10.8 g, Protein: 2.8 g.

Avocado Wedges

Prep Time: 10 minutes/ Cook Time 8 minutes/ Serves: 2

Ingredients:

- 1 avocado, cut into 8 wedges
- ¼ cup all-purpose flour
- ¼ cup panko bread crumbs
- 1 large egg
- ½ tbsp. water
- 1 tsp black pepper
- Salt to taste

Directions:

1. Preheat the Ninja Air Fryer to 400 degrees F.
2. Combine the egg and water in a shallow large bowl.
3. Combine the pepper and flour in another shallow bowl.
4. Place the panko breadcrumbs in a third bowl.
5. Dredge the avocado wedges in the flour mixture then the egg wash and finally the breadcrumbs.
6. Air fry the avocado wedges for 8 minutes. Flip the avocado wedges halfway through the cooking process.
7. Sprinkle with salt and serve.

Nutrition value per serving: Calories: 177 kcal, Carbs: 15.6 g, Fat: 11.5 g, Protein: 4.3 g.

BAKED PEAR

Prep Time: 7 minutes/ Cook Time 12 minutes/ Serves: 4

Ingredients:

- 2 pears, peeled, halved and cored
- 2 tbsp. butter, melted
- 1 tsp vanilla extract
- ½ tsp ground cinnamon

Directions:

1. Preheat the Ninja Air Fryer to 350 degrees F.
2. Combine the melted butter, cinnamon and vanilla.
3. Baste the pear with the butter mixture and place cut side down in the air fryer basket.
4. Bake for 10 minutes. Flip the pear, baste with the remaining butter mixture and air fry for 2 minutes.
5. Serve as is or with whipped cream or ice cream.

Nutrition value per serving: Calories: 115 kcal, Carbs: 16.3 g, Fat: 5.9 g, Protein: 0.5 g.

SWEET POTATO FRIES

Prep Time: 2 minutes/ Cook Time 15 minutes/ Serves: 1

Ingredients:

- 1 medium sweet potato, cut into 1/4" thick fries
- 1 tbsp. canola oil
- Salt and pepper to taste

Directions:

1. Preheat the Ninja Air Fryer to 350 degrees F.
2. Toss the sweet potato fries with the rest of the ingredients.
3. Air fry sweet potatoes for 15 minutes then serve with desired toppings or sauce.

Nutrition value per serving: Calories: 114 kcal, Carbs: 11.8 g, Fat: 7.1 g, Protein: 1.2 g.

CINNAMON DONUTS

Prep Time: 15 minutes/ Cook Time 8 minutes/ Serves: 5

Ingredients:

- 3/4 self-rising flour
- 1 cup Greek yoghurt
- 1 tbsp. vanilla extract
- ¼ cup ground cinnamon
- ¼ cup granulated white sugar

Directions:

1. Combine the flour, vanilla extract and Greek yoghurt.
2. Roll out the dough on a floured surface. Divide into 5 and pinch the ends together to form a circle donut.
3. Preheat the Ninja Air Fryer to 375 degrees F.
4. Air fry the donuts for 8 minutes. Flip halfway through the cooking process.
5. Sprinkled doughnuts with a mixture of the sugar and cinnamon.

Nutrition value per serving: Calories: 108 kcal, Carbs: 22.5 g, Fat: 0.8 g, Protein: 2.5 g.

HONEY ROASTED PEANUTS

Prep Time: 2 minutes/ Cook Time 5 minutes/ Serves: 2

Ingredients:

- 1 cup plain peanuts
- 1 tbsp. honey
- 1 tsp salt

Directions:

1. Preheat the Ninja Air Fryer to 350 degrees F.
2. Toss all the ingredients together then lay in a single layer in the air fryer baskets.
3. Air fry for 5 minutes. Shake the basket at least twice.
4. Cool and serve.

Nutrition value per serving: Calories: 62 kcal, Carbs: 9.2 g, Fat: 2.5 g, Protein: 1.2 g.

Pepperoni Chips

Prep Time: 1 minutes/ Cook Time 8 minutes/ Serves: 4

Ingredients:

- 20 pepperoni slices

Directions:

1. Preheat the Ninja Air Fryer to 360 degrees F.
2. Layer the pepperoni at the bottom of the air fryer basket and cook for 8 minutes.
3. Serve with your favorite dipping sauce.

Nutrition value per serving: Calories: 136 kcal, Carbs: 0 g, Fat: 12.1 g, Protein: 6.2 g.

Apple Chips

Prep Time: 7 minutes/ Cook Time 8 minutes/ Serves: 1

Ingredients:

- 1 large crisp apple, sliced into 1/8" rounds
- ¼ tsp ground cinnamon
- A pinch of salt

Directions:

1. Preheat the Ninja Air Fryer to 390 degrees F.
2. Combine the cinnamon and salt in a small bowl. Rub this mixture onto the apple slices.
3. Arrange the apple slices in a single layer in the air fryer basket and cook for 8 minutes. Flip halfway through the cooking process.
4. Cool and serve.

Nutrition value per serving: Calories: 42 kcal, Carbs: 11.3 g, Fat: 0.2 g, Protein: 0.2 g.

Salted Nuts

Prep Time: 2 minutes/ Cook Time 8 minutes/ Serves: 4

Ingredients:

- ½ cup cashew nuts
- ½ cup almonds
- Olive oil
- Salt and pepper to taste

Directions:

1. Preheat the Ninja Air Fryer to 350 degrees F.
2. Toss all the ingredients together and layer the nuts at the bottom of the air fryer basket. Cook for 6 minutes. Shake the basket halfway through the cooking process.
3. Serve.

Nutrition value per serving: Calories: 175 kcal, Carbs: 8.2 g, Fat: 14.8 g, Protein: 5.1 g.

CONCLUSION

In conclusion of this book, I would like to thank you for reading my work and I hope that you have come to the realization that you can lose weight and live healthily while still enjoying the fried foods that you love most. Fried foods are known for their delicious flavor but they also have a bad reputation for putting extra pounds around your waistline. Most diets strictly prohibit or entirely exclude fried foods from the diet but finally there is a way that you can still continue to enjoy the delicious flavor of fried foods while still maintaining a healthy weight.

The Ninja Air Fryer is the cutting edge tool that allows you to continue to eat fried food without the negative health consequences, one of which is weight gain. It allows everyone to enjoy the crisp outside yet juicy and soft inside of fried foods without all the grease. It also cooks, reheats, broils and dehydrates food fast and easy.

The aim of this book was to educate you on how you can use this tool to simplify your life while living healthy. I hope that you use the delicious recipes outlined inside to not only delight your taste buds but to also control your weight.

Lightning Source UK Ltd.
Milton Keynes UK
UKHW052346291021
393078UK00006B/415